Copyright ©2020, Macy Fuller

ALL RIGHTS RESERVED.

No part of this publication may be reproduced, stored in a retrieval system, or transmitted in any form or by any means—electronic, mechanical, photo-copy, recording, or any other—except for brief quotation in reviews, without the prior permission of the author or publisher.

ISBN: 978-1-60414-702-5

Published by

Fideli Publishing, Inc.
119 W. Morgan St.
Martinsville, IN 46151
www.FideliPublishing.com

Unlocking the darkness to open the path of healing.

Table of Contents

Childhood 1

High School Years.. 19

Leaving Home 33

My Life After Military Service 63

Another Chance.. 83

Mom 99

The Will to Live.. 115

My Revelation 117

ME (Lyrics).. 121

demoralized
disappointment
guilt
frustrated
mental abuse
anger
loneliness
depression
mad
sick
shame self-hate dirty
disbelief grief numbness
self-hate
sadness hurt worried
depression suffocated fear of people
hate alone pain self-blame
disgust anger
miserable low self-esteem
avoidance
lack of energy
emotional abuse
physical abuse

Author's Note

I believe the book "Me" was put on my heart by God to write as a healing process for me and to help someone else to overcome some struggles that they are facing. While in the process of writing this book, I came to realize that part of me was left in each traumatic experience as if I was put in a dark room by myself with no windows and no way out.

The part of me that left my body and watched all these things happen moved on, which left me feeling empty. The only way for me to feel whole was to go back and reconnect the pieces. I am not going to lie, it felt like a suicide mission at first.

All the emotions that came at me were like a hurricane, tornado, earthquake, tsunami and volcano — all at once. I felt like I was losing control. I was screaming and no one could hear me. There was no clapping your heels together three times like Dorothy in *The Wizard of Oz*.

This was real life. I tried to escape again and move on, but I hated the way things were: the emptiness, the not being able to connect, and the feeling of just existing. I decided to push forward. Yes, kicking and screaming, like a newborn baby entering the world.

I can't emphasize how important it is to get help so you can start the healing. Doing it alone is too hard. That brings me to the therapist that helped me — she is amazing. I honestly don't think I could have gone through this without her. I gave up several times but she kept on guiding and coaching me every step of the way.

I have learned so much and I am still learning. For example, I have learned that forgiveness is easy to say but actually forgiveness is hard to do. For those of you who say, "just get over it and move on," I want to tell you it's like you are paralyzed and everyone is yelling at you to get up and do something. You want to, but you can't until you are taught to move again. That's how I feel. Here is the beginning of my story, *ME*.

demoralized
guilt dirty
Miserable
loneliness Depression
frustrated Self-blame
Self-hate disconnect
Abuse anger disgust
Physical Abuse
Emotional Abuse
Mental Abuse
fear of people
feeling stupid
suffocation

Childhood

When I was a little girl, I was full of life. I was extremely active and creative, or so I was told. What did my mom expect from me — after all, when I was born, I was born breach? I came out butt first, so basically, I came out telling the world to kiss my butt. That should have been a clue to her that I was going to be a handful.

I got into everything and I do mean everything; for example, one time after my mom ironed her clothes, she went to take a bath and then the creativity began. Curiosity got the best of me. I noticed that I had wrinkles on my stomach, and of course I had to iron them out. No one told me that fat rolls weren't wrinkles.

We are talking about me. I stuck the iron to my stomach. I went from barely walking right into running a marathon. I ran screaming and jumped into the bathtub with my mom.

She didn't know what was wrong with me, until she saw the blisters bubble up on my stomach. I still have that scar on my stomach — it looks like a tattoo gone wrong. Oh, yeah, I might add that I also have a weird sense of humor as well.

Talk about creativity, I had imaginary friends. Each one of my imaginary friends had names. One of their names was Whoochie. My imaginary friends would talk, play and even fight with me. On one occasion, I was eating at the kitchen table by myself and my mom heard a big thump. She found me crying and getting off the floor. When my mom asked me what happened, I said my imaginary friend pushed me out of my chair.

My mom said it always sounded like I had a house full of kids playing with me. She was worried about me and asked the doctor if I was okay. She told the doctor that my imaginary friends and I would spend hours and hours of time together. The doctor told her that I was normal, and that I just needed siblings.

My mom was married but not to my father. My stepfather treated me kindly, as if he was my real father. Once when his mom, my grandmother, was piercing my ears I was screaming from the top of my lungs. He rushed in the house asking what they were doing to his baby. He always showered me with love. He never mistreated me. He even wanted to adopt me, but his mother said no, because if my mother would ever leave, he would be financially responsible for me.

My mother and stepfather were having problems and my mother left him and moved back to Muncie, Indiana. We lived in Anderson, Indiana, at the time.

When we moved back to Muncie, we lived across the street from my biological father's mother. My grandmother did not play and no one messed with her. She sold ice cream cones in the neighborhood. I would go across the street and buy ice cream but she would never take my money. She was always so nice to me and would often ask how I was doing. I think she reported back to my dad because one time I had a black eye and my dad came around and asked my mom what happened to my eye. I had gotten stung in the eye by a bee.

I never called her grandma but I would tell all the kids that she was my grandma. One of my dad's sisters heard me tell a kid my dad's name and she yelled at me telling me that her brother was not my dad. From that day forward, I always saw her as an evil old witch. What kind of adult verbally attacks a kid — hence the name evil old witch. My biological father wasn't around for much of my childhood nor did he ever support my mom financially. I saw him here and there.

My mom met a man. He was much, much older than she was. He was well known and respected in the community. The relationship lasted for approximately fifteen or more years, give or take.

We had moved from across the street from my biological dad's mom into an apartment close to the elementary school that I would later attend. We lived with the well-known man and, basically, he took care of us. At least that's what I remembered. They had a son together. Bye-bye imaginary friends; hello, my bratty little brother. My brother and I are six years apart.

With my imaginary friends gone, I had to find new friends. A few blocks over from where we lived, I met one of my biological dad's brothers, his wife and their two daughters. I would visit them frequently — I think I would go over their house every day — but my memory is a little foggy on that.

One day they told me they were leaving Indiana and moving to, I think, California. They were gentle in the way they delivered that news to me, but nevertheless I was crushed. I really loved them so much and they were so kind. I remember after they left, I would walk by the house that they lived in, longing for them to be there. I had no way of getting in touch with them.

I was left to play with my little brother, which was no fun because my brother and I would fight all the time. He was a brat and he moved fast. He was always doing something and never got in trouble. I always kept my eye on him, so I could tell on him to get him in trouble.

We shared a bedroom. One time he tried to set our room on fire. He started a fire in our bedroom then he shut the door. I saw him shut the door quickly. I opened the door and saw the fire. We were able to get the fire out before it did any damage.

After we put the fire out my, mom was going to give him a whooping but she couldn't catch him. She had me help to try to catch him. We cornered him in the kitchen and he ran under the kitchen table and out the front door. He never got that whooping.

At that time, we had a dog name Chopper, and I am sure my brother could outrun Chopper. I think we named the dog Chopper because he would chase people and bite at their ankles, but he wouldn't really bite them, or maybe he got his name from some cartoon we used to watch.

My mom started working at a janitorial job. My aunt, my mom's baby sister, would babysit us while my mom worked. The well-known man would give my brother and me money, so that we could walk to Clark gas station to buy candy. I would always wonder why she couldn't come with us. She was a kid, too, and she liked candy. She was in her early teenage years.

One day my aunt told everyone that the well-known man was making sexual advances on her, but no one listened. My mom's dad was the only one that listened, and he was mad about it. He couldn't do anything about it because he couldn't walk — he had been in a train accident that really messed him up. All the other family members acted like nothing ever happened.

My mom's job caused arguments between her and the well-known man, and she eventually quit the job. They argued all the time in the house. Finally, my mom left him and we moved to Grand Rapids, Michigan.

In Michigan, I would go to church with one of my great aunts. I loved it and I even got saved. I felt like a new person because I had accepted Jesus in my life. I tried really hard to be a good girl and live like the Bible said.

We lived in this apartment that looked nice, but at night there were roaches everywhere. Those roaches were having a "Family Reunion." They were catapulting from the ceilings, having a house party. The kids at school would make fun of me teasing me saying we live in the house that had the "gangster" roaches.

We moved shortly after that. I liked our new apartment. The kids were nice and I had older friends that looked out for me. We played Double Dutch jump rope from the time we woke up until the time we went to sleep. I enjoyed the school we went to. I was even a crossing guard at the school.

My mom was dating a man who moved in with us. I remember him as the man with the green eyes or maybe they were hazel. When he left, he stole everything we owned, which wasn't much, just TVs and a stereo. My mom wasn't doing too well, I guess, because within a year we moved back to Muncie. She got back with the well-known and respected man. We had moved in with him. My brother and I shared a bedroom.

That's when things changed for me. My brother and I witnessed physical fights between our mother and the well-known man. There was lots of yelling, screaming and fighting constantly. One minute my mom would have the gun, chasing the well-known man, then the next minute he would have the gun. While I would be crying and screaming, they would yell at me, telling me to shut up and to go in the bedroom with my brother and shut the door.

If it wasn't the guns, it was the knives. I felt like I was a basket case. Sometimes my mom would come in the bedroom to get us, telling us that we were leaving, and the well-known respected man would come in behind her telling us to stay. They would fight right in front of us. To this day I can't stand to hear people arguing or yelling — it makes me extremely nervous and triggers emotional distress. I freak out every time and I need to leave. I try to hide it; sometimes I can pull it off and other times I have a complete melt down.

* * *

When I got my period, I didn't know what had hit me. It was early in the morning. My brother made fun of me laughing and running to tell our mom that I had peed in the bed, when in fact I had wet the bed trying to clean it. I was a tomboy. I wasn't ready for that crap. I had to deal with boobs and now this.

I thought I was going to get in trouble. I nervously told my mom what happened and asked her what to do. My mom sent me walking to the store to buy the pads. At the store, I was so lost. I felt so overwhelmed because there were too many pads to choose from. I could imagine myself standing there screaming I just want some pads for arts and crafts at panty camp and then bursting into tears. "Arts in crafts at panty camp" is just a code name used for the dreaded monthly period.

My mom told the well-known man that I had got my period, soon after things changed so drastically. The unthinkable started.

I can't remember the exact time, the how or even the why. I would wake up with his hands in my panties and he would tell me to be quiet. I would push him away and fight him off. He only stopped because I don't think he wanted to wake my brother up. He would have this weird smirk on his face when he walked away. Here this man that I considered my stepfather, who had been part of most of my young life, was doing things to me.

I was so angry and shaken up over what had happened. I was told I couldn't tell anyone because everyone would call me fast and judge me. It would ruin my life. He would tell me that he was all I had, that nobody else is going to take care of me, and that my real daddy didn't want me. He would tell me that my family was "ass backwards and the women in my family had whorish ways." I believed him when he said nobody else would take care of me and that my real daddy didn't want me.

I thought my mother hated me because she hated my daddy. I had ruined her life because I wasn't planned and she was left to take care of me by herself at a young age. She would look at me sometimes like I made her sick. My family never took the kid's side on anything so I kept quiet.

These encounters were frequent and started progressing into more than just hands in my panties fondling me. He was taking more interest in me. He was teaching me how to fight, have me watch boxing with him. He would teach me about how to save money, try to help me with my schoolwork. By the way, I got an "F "on the school work when he helped.

He was overly protective of me. One time I lied and told him that one of his sons tried to hit on me. He jumped all over his son. I thought he was going to hurt him. My mom stepped in to protect his son. I felt really bad that I told that lie and I never apologized to his son. I had a hard time understanding why it was ok for him to do things to me but not anyone else and why my mom was so loving to everyone except me.

As time went on, I kept the sexual abuse to myself and it continued to happen more and more. I would ask God why and how could he let bad things happen to little kids. I remember I would pray to God to make him stop, and I prayed for him to die, but that didn't happen.

I learned how to separate from my body, while the sexual abuse happened. I could see myself looking down at myself. It was like I went to another world and I would stay there until he was finished. I really felt bad about myself, about me wishing death on someone, so I made my first attempt at suicide.

I started taking a bottle of Tylenol in the bathroom. I took maybe five and then I stopped and went into the front room where he was. I asked him what would happen if I took a bunch of Tylenol. He told me I better not and I listened. I didn't take any more, and instead I started creating sores on my hands and arms by using my fingernails as a knife or taking a pencil eraser and rubbing my skin off. No one noticed.

Everyone said my brother and I were spoiled because he got us everything. What no one knew was everything that I needed and wanted had a string attached to it. Part of me hated him and part of me loved him because he was the only father I had. He would always refer to me as his daughter, not his stepdaughter.

I needed an outlet or I would try to commit suicide again, so I started writing songs and I auditioned for ballet at Muncie Ballet Theater. I made the cut, so I got to take free dance lessons. In my mind, I thought I would get rich and I wouldn't have to depend on anyone. That would solve my problems and everyone would love me.

I was excited when we were going to have our first ballet recital. They gave us ten tickets to sell, and I remember I turned all ten tickets back in, because no one bought any tickets from me. I was so devastated, especially when the teacher had stated the obvious, "your parents aren't coming." I told her my stepfather dropped me off and would pick me up later. It really bothered me and I felt all alone. I loved dancing so much. I never returned back to ballet; after all, what was the point no one cared.

I then focused on songwriting. My very first song that I wrote was called "Playgirl." I sent it into Sunrise Records and they replied back with a contract and fee amount for studio time. Again, I was so excited I thought for sure this was it.

believe in yourself   dream it and do it   Make Things HAPPEN

dream   inspire

live   create
     love
  hope   laugh

face the Music

My mom didn't want any part of it, so I begged my stepfather and he told me I know what I had to do if I want him to signed and pay the fee. I cried and begged and his reply was still the same, so I agreed. I knew the routine by now because it was happening so frequently. I told myself I could just go to my happy place and then it will be over.

My recorded record came back and I thought my mom would be so proud that I had made a record. Well, she wasn't. She hated it because it wasn't the type of music that they listened to at that time. They were not open to any other music type other than what they listened to.

There was another contract and additional fees for distribution of the record again, I begged but mom didn't want any part of it. My stepfather was going to sign and pay for it as long as I agreed to his terms, but I refused and things got ugly around the house.

I was getting into trouble all the time. He even gave me a whooping with a belt because my brother hit me and I hit him back. We always fought and normally we just got yelled at, but this particular time I got a whooping.

I hated my life. I kept writing songs and tried really hard to get good grades so they would be proud of me. My brother and I fought, but I didn't hit him while they were home. He would throw rocks and hit me in the head, or hit me in the head with belt buckles. That little brat always went for my head. I had one

aiming for my head and the other for my crotch — nothing was safe.

Once on our way to school, my brother rammed into me on a hill. I went flying through the air and when I landed, I was dazed. Once I got to school, I was sent home, and I had to walk by myself. At home, my mom just had me to lie down.

Life for me was sucky, but I continue to write my songs. I learned that I could be in my happy place even when I wasn't being violated sexually. Most of the time I could tune out the negative words my mom and people said to me because I would go to my happy place.

In my happy place I found peace and comfort. I could change who I was and erase all the bad things away. There was a presence there that protected and spoke to me, not with words like people talk to each other, but it spoke to my soul. That is how I made it through most of my pre-teen and teen years.

Mom and the well-known man were having problems still and mom finally moved out and found us a place of our own. The well-known man still had control over our life even though we did not live with him.

My mom was so picky. She always had to have things spotless — it couldn't just be straightened up, it had to be cleaned. We had the basics but we did not have a washer and dryer. Mom always went over her mom's house to do our laundry.

Since my mom did not drive, sometimes we had to walk with baskets of clothes over to my grandma's house or sometimes people would give us a ride when they saw us walking. I hated that so much because Willard Street was a busy street and everybody saw you, but she was on welfare and she did the best she could. I resented being on welfare so much that I made myself a promise never to be on welfare.

In 1981 or 1982, a man gave us a ride over my grandma's house so my mom could do our laundry. Well, let's call the man Mr. L. I think Mr. L liked Mom and maybe they were trying to sort of date. I am not sure what was really going on with those two.

While we were over my grandma's, I think Mom and Mr. L were in the kitchen talking, and Mom might have gone into the basement to start a load of clothes. The well-known man must have seen Mr. L's car and he decided to stop by. He came in the back door which led right in the kitchen. The well-known man called my brother and me into the kitchen. As soon as we stepped foot into the kitchen, the well-known man started fighting Mr. L and pulled out his gun. The gun went off three times while they wrestled with it.

My brother was gone immediately. Speedy Gonzales was out the door and gone. I, on the other hand, I stood frozen screaming, watching it all play out in front of me. I saw them wrestle with the gun. I saw when the well-known man stabbed Mr. L across the face. I just stood there screaming, right in the middle of harm's way.

Mr. L managed to get away. He ran out the kitchen door, got in his car and left with blood dripping from his face. The well-known man left as well. Someone came and got me and took me outside.

I don't remember much from that point on, except the cops showed up. My brother and I never received any counseling, which I believe we should have. My mom and one of my aunts got counseling and they were admitted to a hospital in another city.

Later, when I asked the well-known man why he had called us in the kitchen, he stated he was checking on my brother and me and that he wanted to give us money. I was terrified and I believed the rumors that were said about the well-known man. He never did one ounce of jail time. He could do whatever he wanted and nobody dared to do anything about it. I believe he was sending me a message to ensure my silence.

My mom did start dating again, but not to Mr. L. She started hanging out at this private club and dating someone at the club. My aunts would go out, and I had to babysit. That's when the real fun begins.

I had made my cousins as my band members. They were my backup singers. If they didn't cooperate, I made them stand in the corner with their hands up with books on their hands. I always loved music and writing songs and now I had part of a band.

I found out later that my cousins hated coming over my house. They made up a song about me. It went like this: "When you come to Macy's house, she don't treat you right." My cousin told me that they would cry and sing this song.

My mom started dating someone else from that private club. She stayed a week at a time over his house, leaving me to take care of my brother and myself. She would always say, you have the number if you need me.

The well-known man did not like that at all and he would argue with her, telling her no good mother leaves her kids to stay with a man, but she didn't see anything wrong with that. On one of their arguments, my mom left our house and went across the street to her sister's house. I had a dog named Princess; we always had a dog. Well, Princess followed my mom across the street and got hit by a car. Princess's leg was hurt badly, her skin was hanging off, and she couldn't walk. I got a blanket and gently put her on it. I was crying so hard. I begged them to take her to the vet. Princess was crying and I was crying.

The well-known man said it would cost too much, but he looked at me and I knew what he was implying. I shook my head yes in agreement. We took Princess to the vet and they took care of her, updated her shots and everything.

Yes, it was expensive, but my dog lived. The well-known man continued to look out for my brother and me. He would stop by frequently to give us money and if we needed anything, he would take care of what we needed. In return I had to come over his house to pay the debt back.

High School Years

In high school I met some cool friends. I didn't have a big group, but I had the best groups. I say groups because I hung out with them separately. At school I met a girl and her sister who could sing. We called ourselves a singing group and it was fun. I wrote a song for us to sing and we would practice a lot. I just knew we were going places. I think we were going to try out for our talent show at school. I don't think we did and I am not sure what happened.

During that time, I became friends with another girl who had an amazing voice. She loved her some Prince. She sang the lyrics to two of my songs and she put it on a cassette. I was going to send it to Sunrise records to see if they would record it the way she sang it.

We hung out after school and we talked about music. I didn't hang out much or even long because I had to be in before dark — rules of the well-known man. I couldn't even attend the school games.

The girl that could sing. I had gotten close, too. I felt comfortable enough to share that I attempted suicide but I never told her why. She told me if I ever felt like that again, I should call her. I am not sure why we stopped hanging out. It might have been because school was out and I had taken on a summer job to help my mom out or maybe because I slowly leave people, keeping them at a distance.

The story about how I got this summer job was so funny. I was walking down the busy Willard Street, most likely coming from my grandma's house and a man tried to hit on me. He said, "Hey, what's your name."

I told him my name. I wasn't interested in him — he was actually annoying me, and he knew it, but he continued to talk to me. He wanted to know my last name, and I told him.

You see, Muncie is small, and everybody knows everybody especially in the black community. When I told him my last name, he said, "Oh, you're that smart Ellis girl."

He also knew of my stepfather, the well-known man. He stopped trying to hit on me, and he said he had someone he wanted me to meet. He said she was a positive role model for smart young girls like me. He said, she will love you her name is Alice. He gave me information for me to contact her and said he would tell her about me. That summer I had signed up for a summer job that she happened to be in charge of, and yes, he did tell her about me.

Meanwhile, I had gone by my biological dad's mom's house and I asked her how I could get in touch with my dad. She looked at me and said, "I am going to give you his number, but don't tell him I gave it to you, because of his wife."

I called and his wife answered the phone, he wasn't home. We argued for a minute, and then we hung up. Later, that day my father called back because his wife told him that I wanted to talk with him. He said he would come to Muncie and we could talk. He lived in Richmond.

Mom wasn't home when he showed up. I went outside and sat in his truck. He didn't want to come in. I looked him straight in his eyes and said, "I have been told all my life you were my father, and if you don't think you are my father, can we please do a blood test so we can know?"

He looked at me and said, "I don't need a blood test. You are my daughter."

When I asked him why he hasn't been a part of my life, he said it was complicated. He started coming to see me and he took me clothing shopping. He got me a moped. It felt so nice not to have strings attached. I had my real father. He did care about me.

It was sort of awkward, because I had loved this man all my life, and we didn't really know each other. I didn't know his favorite color, what foods he liked. He asked me to come stay the summer with him, and I got to hang around my half-sisters.

I wanted to stay with him because I wanted to get to know him better. I had asked them if I could live with them and my stepmom said your mom is not going to let you live with us. I told them that she would if I told them something. It's something really bad. She said I was lying before I even said anything, so I didn't say anything. Also, I didn't want anything bad to happen to my dad.

My summer with my dad was cut short because the summer job came through and I had to come back home to work. Alice M. had me work in the office with her. She was amazing and smart. It was an honor to be around her. I learned so much from her.

My father continued to see me. Mom and the well-known man did not like that. One morning, I was running late for work because a bird had gotten into the house somehow, and I am terrified of birds. My cousin and I had to get the bird out, so I could get dressed for work. My mom was over at her boyfriend's house. I wrecked my moped trying to hurry to get to work on time, but I was ok.

I guess that was the straw that broke the camel's back. My mom went off on my father, and she had him take the moped back with him. She was so mean to him. After that, it was like he didn't want anything to do with me.

* * *

At the end of the summer job program, Alice M. had taken us on a learning field trip out of state. We went to Atlanta, Georgia. We learned about Martin Luther King. We got to visit places about him. It was an amazing experience.

I also found out on that trip in Atlanta that the well-known man's girlfriend was pregnant by him. She was in the summer program. She wasn't that old — she might have been in her early twenties. She told me I was going to have a little sister. Summer was over and back to school.

As I was getting older, I started what some might call rebelling, but I call it "taking back control over my life." I wanted to go to the movies with this guy I had a crush on. My mom said I could go and I had arranged for someone to watch my brother.

When it came time for the guy to pick me up, the well-known man showed up. I hid inside the house and never answered the door. I knew if I had gone outside the guy would have been dead and I didn't want any part of that. The guy was mad at me for standing him up. I felt really bad but I couldn't tell him the reason.

My oldest cousin came to live with us because she kept running away. All my mother did was fuss at us all the time. Over the years, I learned not to be present but my cousin did not know how to deal with it. The guy that I had a crush on wanted to meet my mom, so he said. My cousin told the guy not to ever meet my mom because she was a mean witch. That made him scared of her.

One day, my cousin didn't come home from school, so my mom and I walked to the multi-center. My mom had a belt and whipped her with it in front of everyone. My cousin ran all the way home. I felt bad for her. My mother was mean. I understand why now, but I didn't back then.

* * *

I was always embarrassed about being poor. If we didn't have something, we would get it from my grandma if she had it. Once she had me walk over to my grandma's house to get something embarrassing, probably a plunger or toilet paper, I don't really remember.

The guy I had a crush on saw me and asked me where I was going. I told him over my grandma's house. He offered me a ride, and I got in the car with him. He was teasing me about being out when it was getting dark outside.

We rode around and then we went over to his brother's house where he was house sitting. We didn't go over to his house because he lived next door to the well-known man. I slept with him. I didn't like it and I told him I didn't like it. His reply was, at first you won't like it, but later you will. I told myself, at least I picked who I would sleep with.

When he drove me home, I didn't look at him and I just wanted to get far away from him, but he grabbed me as I was getting out of the car and kissed me. I went into the house and took a bath and went to sleep.

The next day Mom was fussing at me and she asked where did I go. I told her, and I told her I slept with the guy I had a crush on. He had called while she was fussing at me, and I told him I would call him back. She was so mad at me but I didn't care. I felt like my life had been crappy for most of my life anyway. I didn't hear the end of it. She made sure she threw that in my face every chance she got.

I continued to rebel even more. I had gotten involved with one of the security guards at the high school. He was also a police officer. My mom threatened to bring him up on charges if he ever came around me again.

I had confided in my best friend at the time about the guy I had a crush on and the security guard. She had been and still is one of my best friends since grade school. Although I don't keep in touch with her, I still think of her as one of my best friends. We mainly hung out at school and called each other on the phone, occasionally I went over her house. She didn't go to parties. Her father was a preacher.

She knew a lot about me, but she didn't know everything about me. I never shared with her the sexual abuse or the suicide attempt. We would ride the city bus to school together and when she got her license, she would pick me up and take me to school. We were late for school a lot. Come to think of it, I never gave her gas money. She never complained about it or even asked. She never put me down — calling me crazy doesn't count.

One time it was storming out and she dropped me off from school. When I went into the house, no one was home, and she had already driven off. I took the phone into the closet and called her to ask her to pick me back up to take me over to my grandmother's house, which was two blocks from her house. She wouldn't because it was storming really bad, so I asked to speak to her mother, and her mother made her come back to get me. We still laugh about it still to this day.

*　*　*

When it came time for me to get my license, the well-known man tried to help me. I think I had taken driver's ed in school, and I had passed the class but I still needed more practice driving. Every time the well-known man would take me out for driving lessons, it would be a disaster. I would come back in tears because he would always yell at me while teaching me to drive.

One particular time when he yelled at me, I slammed on the brakes so hard that we both were jerked forward. The seat belt pulled us backward — it's a wonder our necks weren't broken or we didn't suffer from whiplash. I put the car in park in the middle of the street, and I got out and started walking home. He was driving the car yelling at me to get back in the car. I ignored him and when I got home, I slammed the door behind me.

My mom was home and she asked me what was wrong with me. At that moment the well-known man came in the house. I yelled, "Him," pointing at the well-known man. I ran into my room and slammed the door. I heard him tell my mom that I had a bad attitude.

My mom was still dating the man from the private club. He ended up breaking her nose. At that time I made up my mind that I would not let a man beat up on me, that I would fight him back and I wouldn't fight fair. I would use or do whatever it took to protect myself. My grandma had eight girls. Their boyfriends were always beating them up.

* * *

I was finally old enough to get a real part-time job. The school had a program where you went to school half a day and worked the other half. I had an interview with JCPenney in the mall. I had asked the well-known man if he would take me to my interview and he agreed. However, he made me late. I was in tears, because I really wanted a job so I could take care of myself. I was tired of depending on him for help. Luckily, I got the job.

I didn't work at JCPenney long. Alice M. had gotten me a job at the social security office. She continued to look out for me even after the summer job was over.

My aunt who is exactly ten years older than I am had the best clothes. She had way too many clothes, shoes, and accessories. Anything you needed, she had it. She loved shopping and I could fit into her clothes and shoes. I would go over my grandma's house where she lived and she would let me try on her clothes, resulting in my wearing her clothes. Sometimes I got to keep them and sometimes I just didn't return them. Her room was like a department store. You can't blame me; I had a job and I needed to look nice.

I looked up to her because she had a job and her own car. I saw she was doing something with her life. She was the only one out of all my aunts who had her driver's license. I hadn't gotten my license yet because I needed a car to use. She let me use her car one day before she had to go to work. Her car was a Corsica.

The BMV had just moved to their new location. It was a mess with a lot of road construction in the area. I had passed the written test and I was ready for the driving portion. We had been sitting forever, and I had to ask the driving instructor if I could take the driving portion soon because we had been there for a long time and my aunt had to go to work and I wouldn't have a car to use.

The driving instructor looked mad. He didn't say much to me at all. He had me drive a couple of blocks around the corner and then park back at the BMV. I didn't know if I had passed or not. When we went in the BMV my aunt asked if I had passed and he said yes. I was so happy.

High School Years

To this day I tell people I got my license from Kmart. I can't drive worth a darn. I can't parallel park or back up that good. All that mattered was I had my license.

Sometimes my aunt would let me use her car, but not for long — maybe just to run to the store and back. She was dating this man, and he had made a pass at me. At the time I thought it was because he had been drinking too much, but when he wasn't drinking, he propositioned me. He said if I would go to the motel with him, he would give me money to buy a car.

I turned him down but he continued to ask and sweetened the deal and I continued to decline his offer. He didn't deserve my aunt — she was too good for him. It made me sick to think he would do that to her and I was still a kid. He had kids my age. After all that I had been through, my opinion of men was very low. It made me have low tolerance for men.

* * *

I started dating a guy from Central High School — did I mention I went to Southside High School? His mother was one of my teachers in high school. It was kind of awkward dating him and having her as my teacher.

One day I wore his letterman jacket to school and this girl who he was supposed to be dating or liking came up to me. I really don't know the story about that and I never asked. We talked and later we found out that our mothers knew each other, and they were friends. The guy and I ended up breaking up. I think he was going away to college and there was an issue with the well-known man.

I really can't remember all the details; nevertheless, the girl became one of my best friends. I still had my other best friend from grade school. This girl and I started hanging out and she introduced me to her sisters and her friends. We started going to parties. We were doing the normal teenage stuff.

By this time, I was having very little contact with the well-known man because I could take care of myself and he couldn't hold anything over my head, except when it came time for me to get my stuff for my senior year. I couldn't afford everything that I thought I needed. He helped get my class ring, senior pictures, cap and gown. That help came with a cost. I knew the routine, but that was the last time I asked him for help.

The girl that I started hanging out with and going to parties with lived around the corner from where I lived. We would walk up and down Willard Street like we owned it. It was so funny because we knew we were all that and we dared anyone to mess with us.

On one of our walks an older man approached me. He was a friend of my aunt that had the department store in her room. They had gone to school together. I knew him fairly well and we started dating.

Although he was much older than me, no one had a problem with him dating me, not even my mother. I would sometime drive his car to school, help him manage his finances.

At first we seem like a good team. He was always around. He would come over to my house and help out around the house, run errands for my mom. We would be watching TV together and I would fall asleep while watching TV with him. He would wake me up to let me know he was going home and to make sure that I would lock the door behind him.

Things were going fairly good until one day I was driving his car. I had dropped him off at work and on my way back home I got pulled over. I had no clue on why I was being pulled over. When the officer told me the plates were expired, I was shocked because I had helped him with managing his money and bills.

The officer allowed me to drive the car home. When he got off work, I questioned him about his plates and that's when I found out he was doing drugs. I warned him that I couldn't and wouldn't date anyone on drugs. He assured me he would stop. I believed him and I offered him support.

Everything was going well until he got me an engagement ring. I wore it to school and this girl saw the ring on my finger as she walked by while I was sitting at my desk. She called me a bitch. I stood up and asked her what did she say and she started to call me a bitch again and I hit her. We fought and were expelled from school.

It almost cost me my high school diploma because we were kicked out of school and we were not allowed to make up any missed assignments. Luckily, I had enough credits and had never been in trouble at school before, so I was able to attend my graduation.

I found out why she had called me a bitch. My fiancé had dated her before me and he had been talking with her on the phone about me. I was going to break up with him and he begged me not to break up with him. He said nothing was going on, that she had called him and they were just talking on the phone casually. I gave him another chance until I found out he was still doing drugs. He left me no choice; I had to break up with him.

He continued to try to get me to stay with him. My friend and I were walking down Willard Street one day like we always did and he started following behind us trying to get me back. We would yell at him and I would throw rocks at his car to get him to leave me alone.

I did not take him back. I was making preparation for my life after high school. I was going to move out into an apartment downtown, close to the social security office where I worked in hopes that I would continue to work there and go to college. One of my friends and I were going to share the apartment.

Leaving Home

When I told my mom of my plans of moving out, she went off on me. She said if I moved out and couldn't make it on my own, I couldn't come back to her house. I was crushed. I cried to my baby aunt and told her what my mom had said to me. My aunt told me if I couldn't make it on my own that I could come live with her. To me, the offer was nice, but it just didn't feel right that my own mother would say that to me.

I went ahead and joined the Army. I had considered it previously anyway. The social security office hadn't said if I was going to be able to stay on or not. I had taken the test for the Army, swore into the delayed entry program. Then the social security office finally had gotten back with me on whether or not I would be able to stay on, and they also had offered to pay a portion of college at Indiana Business College.

I immediately contacted the Army recruiter to ask if I can change my mind because I was going to go to college locally for now. The recruiter told me that I couldn't change my mind because I had already sworn in.

I knew I wanted to be a doctor and I knew I couldn't afford college on my own. I told myself instead of wasting money on a business degree to help me finance becoming a doctor; I could jump right in the medical field. The military would help with the cost, so I just went with what the recruiter told me. I didn't tell my mom until the recruiter picked me up that morning to leave to go to the Army.

When she asked where I was going that time of morning with that man, I told her I joined the Army and I was leaving for boot camp now. My mom told me I would never make it in the Army. I think she said I wouldn't make it because I was really girly girly. I had to have my hair and makeup on before I would even step outside and she was hurt that I left her.

While I was in basic training, I sent my mom money home. After all, in basic you can't spend money anyway and I knew she needed help financially. She had a job but it was only paying minimum wage. I felt like the decision I made to go into the military was a good decision. I was taking complete control over my life and my past was just my past.

When I arrived at Fort Dix, New Jersey, for basic training I was in for a total shock. There were people from everywhere getting off the bus. It was total chaos. I was scared, but I was determined that I could do it.

We were lined up like cattle, given shots and uniforms and assigned to barracks. For some reason or another I caught the eye of a particular male drill sergeant and that is where the trouble began. From the moment I got off the bus, this drill sergeant was in my face yelling at me, which at this point was normal — everybody was being yelled at.

The problem began when he started singling me out, calling me in the office behind closed door with no one else in there. He would offer me candy, try to force me to eat or drink with him. When I wouldn't, he demanded and yelled at me, forcing me to do what he asked me to do. He did not let me leave the room until I did what he asked. I remember feeling the hairs on my back stand up.

This went on the whole time during basic training. A female drill sergeant must have noticed because she would tell me she better not catch me or any other female in the male drill sergeant's face. I constantly tried to hide from both drill sergeants but they would single me out.

Once when I received a letter from my ex, which he had sprayed with my favorite male cologne. The female drill sergeant, before handing me the letter, started saying mean hurtful things to me, such as he doesn't want you, you are nobody special. I didn't realize at the time that painful memories from my childhood were creeping up on me.

Those two drill sergeants caused me extreme stress and anxiety. They triggered flashbacks of what had been happening to me back at home with the well-known man and my mother. I started sleepwalking. Luckily, no one reported me. One time while we were in the field, we had to share this little tent with another person (your ranger buddy), and I dug under her and laid on the ground outside the tent.

I was struggling to make it through basic training. When it came time for the night fire, I had to go through it twice because I had freaked out when the guns were going off over our heads and I was the last soldier to make it in. The senior drill sergeant was mad that I was the last one in so he made me do it again. Another soldier gave me some advice on how to get through the night fire drill faster and it worked.

I didn't tell anyone about any of this. One of my roommates knew of the male drill sergeant singling me out to see him behind closed doors. I kept my mouth shut and played it off by laughing when she teased me about it. I didn't know what to do. I was afraid things would escalate and I would be blamed.

I had injured my knee in basic training but I didn't report that either because everyone told me that I could get kicked out on medical and then my mother would have been right. I could not go back home. I had to force myself to go to my happy place and just exist.

When basic training was over, I was so happy. The male drill sergeant called me into a room behind closed doors once again, but this time he congratulated me on completing basic training. I asked him why he singled me out and he admitted he liked me. He let me wear his drill sergeant hat and he let me order him around but I was never to tell anyone about it. I even got to take a picture wearing his drill sergeant hat.

The female drill sergeant came up to me to tell me that she was hard on me because I reminded her of herself and she wanted to make sure I would succeed. Under other circumstances, that probably wouldn't have been a problem but because of my past it was a major problem. I didn't feel safe and it put me on edge creating extreme anxiety.

I went on to my second part of my training, which was called Advanced Individual Training (AIT). AIT was in Fort Sam Houston in Texas. I was put on a plane for the second time in my life, and I soon came to realize that I don't like flying.

In AIT I didn't have any incidents like I did in basic training, which was good. Although I continued to have sleep walking incidents, again no one reported me. No instructors were hitting on me or singling me out.

AIT was different from basic training in that we had a little bit of freedom — we got weekend passes. I dated a guy in AIT. He even gave me an engagement ring. I remember one time a female soldier from New York dyed her hair and it turned out orange. We laughed so hard because we knew she was going to get into so much trouble. We also used to mock some of the training instructors and officers. We would mock the way they act, walked or talked. Some of the soldiers would even sneak out to go to the NCO club.

Once AIT was over you were on your way to what was called Permanent party or duty station. In January 1990 I was to be stationed at Fort Carson in Colorado. This is where I met Mr. Arrogant and I entered into hell and dance with the devil.

I had been assigned a room with another female that had already been there. In the room we had our own private bathroom and a kitchen, which we shared with the joining room. The roommate and I hit it off right off the bat. We got along really well. She introduced me to her friend and we three hung out together.

My roommate had her own car, so we were always doing something or going somewhere. Although my roommate and I got along really well, I had asked the supply sergeant if I could have my own room. I felt like I couldn't live in the same space with my roommate and hang around with my roommate. I needed some time to be myself to process everything and write my songs. The supply sergeant gave me my own room. He told me I could have my own room for now, but if we get other females in, I would have to have a roommate.

I worked at TMC 3 (Troop Medical Clinic) at Butts Airfield. There I was learning a lot about hands-on medical stuff and also not so medical stuff. I got to watch and assist with minor surgeries.

I also got a crash course of what sexual things men like 101, from one of the sergeants in my chain of command. There was no sexual contact or advances, but he explained to me in detail what to do to a man to please him. I learned so much. I guess you want me to tell all, but nope you will have to read it in my next book called "What Sexual Things Men Like 101." Just kidding. Yes, these things really do go on in the military and so much more.

Our barracks had two common areas: one had a vending machine with a pool table, and the other had a TV with couches. The male soldiers always played pool or they hung out around the CQ desk.

The first encounter I had with, let's just call him Mr. Arrogant, occurred when I went to the vending machine. He started saying inappropriate stuff, looking me up and down. All the male soldiers would laugh, including the male CQ. I didn't think it was funny nor did I like him. I thought he was arrogant. It seems like every encounter I had with Mr. Arrogant would be an exchange of argumentative words.

I had met a guy at the TMC where I worked. He was into music and he would go to the studio. I will call him Music Man. Music Man asked me out and I agreed to go out with him.

When Music Man came to the barracks to pick me up, Mr. Arrogant and the male soldiers were hanging out at the CQ desk playing pool. I am not sure what was said to my date, but Mr. Arrogant said something because my date wasn't happy, and he questioned me about him.

There was nothing going on between Mr. Arrogant and myself at that time. There was another guy that was interested in me and he stopped by the barracks to see me, and again Mr. Arrogant and the usual crew was at it again. Mr. Arrogant was sabotaging my dates.

I decided to continue going out with Music Man. Mr. Arrogant was dating. He would be seen with different women. Around March 1990, I had been admitted into the hospital for 24 hours to get my wisdom teeth taken out. Later on, after I got out of the hospital and could leave the barracks, Music Man and I went out to eat at Popeyes. I couldn't really eat anything except mashed potatoes or rice.

While we were sitting at the table eating, we kept hearing "pssst." We started looking around but we didn't know where it was coming from. Out of nowhere, Mr. Arrogant pops up at our table and introduces himself to Music Man. He gives his name to Music Man, looks at me and says, "that's my girl I got it that way."

Then he walks off with the sergeant he was with. I was shocked at what he just did because this wasn't the first time he had said something to Music Man. Music Man was so upset he accused me of having some type of relationship with Mr. Arrogant. I assured him that I wasn't dating Mr. Arrogant.

I explained to him that we were just in the same unit. I never gave Mr. Arrogant any reason to take notice of me. Music Man and I were over before we even started. Mr. Arrogant had sabotaged my date again.

I am sure I shared what happened to me with my two friends (my old roommate and our other friend). Now it was payback time.

We girls had just got back to the barrack, and Mr. Arrogant was getting out of a vehicle with some girl. I decided to make a scene, so I yelled I was through with him and I wanted all my belongings out of his room.

My old roommate and our other friend were laughing. I was giving Mr. Arrogant a taste of his own medicine. He just laughed and said I got him good. He had started dating this female soldier that was in med hold.

I was so relieved he had a steady girlfriend because that meant he would leave me alone. To my surprise the girl he was dating came up to me and introduces herself as Mr. Arrogant's girlfriend. She said she wanted to meet me because her man liked me and she wanted to meet me for herself. I thought that was strange. I was totally wrong: his having a girlfriend didn't stop him.

The time had come where new soldiers were coming into the unit and I ended up with a roommate. My new roommate was a lab tech. She was nice. I begged the supply sergeant to give me my own room again. He told me usually the higher-ranking soldier gets their own room. I bugged him every day. I finally got my room by myself again. It was on the second floor, but I didn't care as long as I had my own room.

I am not sure what happened to Mr. Arrogant's girlfriend, but she was gone. He continued to harass me every time he saw me.

When Mr. Arrogant got his car, it was a stick. He wanted me to go with him to play arcade games, but I told him I don't play those types of games. Then he offered to teach me how to drive a stick.

He seemed different. He wasn't argumentative. Maybe it was because he was by himself. I agreed to let him teach me how to drive a stick. He was very patient and kind when I would grind the shift. He would say it's okay sweetheart and would explain the correct way. He was so gentle, nothing like that arrogant guy. I thought maybe I misjudged him and we started hanging out as friends. I thought he was a nice guy and I felt comfortable with him.

One day he came to my room — I think it was around his birthday, May 27, 1990. He wanted me to have a drink with him to celebrate his birthday. We drank and I end up in bed with him. The next morning, I felt bad and remember crying. He convinced me that I shouldn't feel bad because it was meant to be.

I found out first sergeant had done an inspection on the room next to mine that night, but he never came to my room. We continued to hangout and I confided in him about my childhood sexual abuse and trauma. As we continued to spend time together, he shared some of his childhood stories. I felt a strong connection because of his troubled childhood with his father and my childhood trauma. Eventually he told me he had a daughter, and he was married and that he was in the middle of a divorce.

I was shocked because he didn't behave like a married man with a child — not once. He claimed he was working on getting a divorce, and that he didn't have the money to get the divorce. That was the only reason why he was still married; at least, that's what he told me.

He said he needed to tell me because he had to bring his wife and child to Colorado. He said his wife was mentally ill and didn't have a place to stay and she couldn't care for the baby. I was hurt and felt betrayed, but I told him to go take care of his family.

In a way, I felt some relief, because I could get back to doing me. He moved out of the barracks. Not long after he moved out of the barracks, out of the blue he showed up at my door. He kept coming back to the barracks to see me. I had hung out with some of the guys we had been playing cards, and one of his so-called friends tried to hit on me. He found out about me hanging out and playing cards with the guys. He was so mad at me.

That's the first time I saw up close the possessive side of him. He would pick me up from the barracks and take me out on long romantic rides, and we would have deep meaningful conversation. He gave me body massages. He literally was charming the hell out of me.

He was so so so charming, but he was also dangerous. Let's just say I wouldn't want to be on the bad side of him. If the first sergeant ever claimed he wasn't aware of what was going on with Mr. Arrogant and his behavior, he was aware of it now because Mr. Arrogant's wife tried to harm herself.

The first sergeant was looking for Mr. Arrogant and it came out that he and I were together. He was fully aware. The first sergeant chose to look the other way like before. Mr. Arrogant worked in personnel and he was chummy with the first sergeant.

By the Army Regulation there should have been some consequences. I learned that military picks and chooses what regulation they will enforce. It all depends on who you know and how high their rank is. There were no consequences for him or me.

His wife left and went back to Chicago and he needed my help with his daughter. She was under a year old. He would come pick me up and take me to his apartment and I would help him with his daughter. Once he had gotten drunk and called me at the barrack, he said he needed me and he asked me to see if someone would bring me to his apartment because he needed my help. I would stay at his apartment cook, clean, do laundry for him and his daughter. I would use my money to help him with groceries or whatever he needed my help with. At the time he seemed to be so grateful for my help and he relied on it. I remember him telling me that if the shoe was on the other foot, he would do the same for me.

I never told him that I liked the intimacy but not the actual sex. Sex was always painful but I never told him. I made him think that I enjoyed it. I was having a lot of pelvic and back pain. I end up having a laparoscopy around September 1990. They didn't find anything wrong, but I was told I would have trouble conceiving because my uterus was tilted toward the back.

I was upset about it and I had called one of my aunts and told her about it. I knew one day when the time was right, I would want kids. I continued to have the pelvic and back pain; it was worse and aggravated every time I did sit ups. Mr. Arrogant later sent his daughter home to his mother-in-law. He eventually moved back in the barracks.

In the barracks there was a big mirror on the second floor he would have us to stop in front of it and he would say we would have a beautiful baby. I would tell him we wouldn't because at the time I had no plans on having a baby. I had my goals of becoming a doctor and a famous singer/songwriter.

* * *

Around October 1990 I found out I was pregnant, and that Mr. Arrogant had given me a permanent STD all at the same time. I was devastated, but when I confronted him, he didn't care. He already knew he had it and had been tested and everything. He just failed to tell me. The charming man that I once knew became a monster. He was the devil.

Shortly after I found out about the pregnancy and the STD, the mental abuse started. He would say things like that's why you slept with your mother's boyfriend. You and your mother shared the same man. All his so-called friends were telling me to get an abortion because he was married, that I should have been taking birth control, that it was my fault that I got pregnant. I was treated badly. Everything was blamed on me.

It seemed like I had stepped into the pits of hell. It felt like some kind of Twilight Zone type of crap. It was amazing to me how things worked when it came to women in the military. I was going to take the pregnancy discharge and go back home, but he convinced me to stay in the military.

I was feeling the pressure and the weight of everything. I didn't believe in abortion. How do I go from it be impossible to conceive to being pregnant with a permanent STD? When I later calculated, I was already pregnant when I had the exploratory laparoscopy.

The sergeant I was under was having marital problems. He didn't like me much because I was pregnant by a married man. When I started having migraines, he could care less. I wasn't able to go to sick call because it was at the hospital, and I had to open for sick call at the TMC while the sergeant came in whenever he felt like it.

I had been having the migraine for a few days and the chief warrant officer called me into the office and asked me if I still had the headache, and I answered yes. He said he had been watching me for a few days and he could tell that I was having a migraine. He chewed my sergeant out for not seeing about his soldier and he had the sergeant to take me to the hospital where I got admitted and treated for migraine. This was around November or December 1990. That didn't help my situation — it only made sergeant hate me more.

In January 1991 I called the TMC3 where I was working to notify them that I needed to go to OB sick call because I had started seeing blood with my pregnancy. The OB front desk staff had already talked to the doctor. She was a major and she said she needed to see me.

My sergeant wasn't in yet, so I left a message with the civilian employee. She told me I better get to the TMC or I would be AWOL. I told her I was at OB sick call, and to please tell my sergeant and I hung up.

The previous night Mr. Arrogant and I had gotten into it really bad. I was stressed and scared to death. At that time, I didn't know that was the reason for the spotting.

While I was sitting in the waiting room waiting to be seen, the first sergeant and two other sergeants came into the waiting room. The first sergeant was yelling at me, telling me he had been all over looking for me. I tried to explain what was going on, but he wouldn't listen. He just kept yelling at me and I lost it. I wasn't thinking at this point. I felt like the safety of me and my baby was at stake, and I started yelling and I said something I shouldn't have said. The situation was very bad.

The OB doctor that was going to see me came in the waiting room and pulled rank and told the first sergeant to stand down. She told him this was not healthy for me or the baby, and that she needed to get me calmed down.

She took me in the examining room, calmed me down and checked the baby. Everything was ok with the baby, and she said she was going to talk with the first sergeant.

The first sergeant told her that he didn't want me back in the unit until I had a mental health evaluation. She tried to explain that being pregnant meant my hormones were all over the place and that I didn't need a mental health evaluation.

She was totally against him sending me, but he had me sent away anyway to a mental hospital, the Fitzsimons Army Hospital in Aurora. I was locked up for six days while I was pregnant.

While I was in the mental institution, one of the workers asked me why I was there. I told her what happened. She told me she was going to help me, but I had to do what she said or else my career in the military was over. I attended whatever therapy session they had. They had a craft workshop. I cooperated 100%. Mr. Arrogant, the devil, came to see me, and he said something that made me start to cry. The worker that was helping me told me not to cry, to remember what she told me.

I held back the tears and kept it inside like I did with everything else that had happened to me. Inside I was feeling trapped and helpless. I started just existing again. I had to manage being in and out of my happy place to survive. In my mind I created a different world where I could exist and not feel. That was the only way I would survive.

For the first time, I could relate to people who have been said to be crazy or schizophrenic. What people don't understand is that sometimes it gets confusing between the worlds. It gets hard to manage being in the happy place and reality.

When I was released from the mental institution I returned to my unit. The first sergeant wanted to see me first thing. When I saw him, he stated that he was there for me and that if I needed anything to let him know.

At that moment I felt complete hate for this man. I wanted to jump over the desk and hurt him. He didn't care about me and I didn't like him or respect him, but I kept those feelings inside. I had to go to my happy place.

The downfall of going to the happy place is you have no clue what is going on or said. I got moved from the TMC to the outpatient clinic at the hospital. I walked on eggshells. I felt like my unit was just waiting for me to mess up.

The staff sergeant that was over me told me later, after we became friends, that she didn't want me working in her clinic under her because she was told I was trouble, but she sees I am not like the way the first sergeant had told her. This was the same first sergeant that allowed a married man to run around like a cave man, the same first sergeant that punished a rape victim. I could go on, but it would be pointless.

I stayed in the barracks as long as I could before I had to move out because I was getting too far along in the pregnancy to stay in the barrack. Mr. Arrogant moved with me off-post and the first sergeant didn't have a problem with it.

Mr. Arrogant got custody of his daughter and she lived with us. I saw and witnessed firsthand what Mr. Arrogant was capable of. He had gotten into a fight at the Air Force base with some off-duty military police and walked away untouched. He could pretty much do whatever he wanted and there were no consequences for him. That reminded me so much of the well-known and respected man from my childhood.

After I gave birth to my son, things got worse as the mental abuse progressed into physical abuse. I went to emergency room on post, and the abuse was documented and reported to my unit but still nothing was ever done. Things were so bad. He was basically doing any and everything you could possibly think of to me.

I know you are probably thinking why you didn't just leave. There were several reasons why. I was scared and I knew he wasn't going to let me go. I was his possession. He always got what he wanted. I felt I was damaged and no one would ever want me. I was marked for life: he made sure of that when he gave me a permanent STD. I also had his daughter to think about. She wasn't mine and I had no rights to her. I felt like I had to stay and try to give her some stability, at least that's what I told myself.

Eventually, I did leave him and move to another apartment complex once the lease was up. I never stopped him from seeing or spending time with his son. I didn't want my son to grow up like I did without my father.

Once when he came over to see his son and to let me see his daughter, I had fallen asleep on the couch. While I was asleep, he had answered my phone and argued with a gentleman that I had given my number to. When I awoke, he told me he had answered my phone and that he had talked to my boyfriend. He was upset about it and he did not want me dating anyone. He didn't want anyone else to raise our son.

He set the ground rules. He was so angry and he didn't care about life. He often referred to himself as the devil and he didn't believe in God.

I felt sorry for him. I let him move in with me once again. After everything I had been through, I was still kind and compassionate. I tried to show him that everyone is not evil and that there are people that are genuinely good.

At first, I thought he was starting to see that with me. We would cook together, laugh, talk, and play with the kids at the park. He was charming and romantic. Out of nowhere, he changed; he went back to the same old stuff — the cheating, the mental abuse and the physical abuse.

The stress took a toll on me. I had started sleepwalking again. At first, we both thought the apartment was haunted because weird stuff was happening, such as all our covers were taken off our bed while we were asleep and put onto the treadmill in the front room. He later told me that he had watched me when I had a sleepwalking episode and he followed me and even had a conversation with me. He said he couldn't make sense of what I was saying, and of course I don't remember any of it, except I would see evidence of what I had done, such as the covers being moved into the other room. The sleepwalking episode scares me because I have no control over what I do.

Finally, I was getting tired of dealing with living like this, so I threatened to leave him and take his daughter and my son with me. He had grabbed me and started choking me, telling me he hated me and that he should kill me.

When I looked in his eyes, I knew he meant it. The only thing that stopped him was his friend that was over visiting him. His friend was also a high-ranking soldier that was in our unit. If he had not been there, he would have killed me. He had his hand around my neck choking me. It hurt so bad to see that much hate and rage in a man that I have done nothing to but show love and support.

The realization that no one loved me hit so hard, and the words that the well-known man said came rushing back. All I could hear is no one loved me, not even my own father, not even my own mother. I was all alone. I felt like life was drained out of me. At that moment, I wished he would have ended my life. I said that when I went to the emergency room on post. This incident was also documented and report to our unit.

Again, there was no intervention from my unit. He called me later on to apologize and he said he was really sorry. That I didn't deserve that and he talked about how his kids needed him. I let him come back. I guess I wanted to believe he meant it.

When he came back, I let him have sex with me. I craved the intimacy because I felt all alone. I really felt like no one really loved me.

I continued to stay with him and nothing changed. My self-esteem had hit rock bottom a long time ago. There were medical issues with my son and my unit wasn't kind about it either. I was told I wasn't supposed to cry in uniform when my son was crying for me while he was being stuck with needles in his spine.

My son had lots of appointments with doctors trying to figure out what was wrong with him. I heard constantly the army didn't issue you any kids when I had to take my son to all kinds of appointments and when I would break down and cry because I couldn't help my baby. I heard the phrase "suck it up" so many times.

During that time, I had gotten orders to go overseas. I had to have my orders to go overseas deferred because of my son's health issues. Truth be told, I believe my son's health problems stemmed from all the stress and complication I had when I was carrying him and the traumatic delivery. I haven't explained everything about the rest of that pregnancy or the complications during delivery because it's such a long story.

I ended up marrying Mr. Arrogant. I didn't care anymore. I was just going through the motion. However, I did reach out to my father to let him know that I had gotten married in hopes that he would be interested in my life and my family. He did make somewhat of an attempt when we visited Muncie. He came to see us, and he brought his grandson a dinosaur toy.

My family liked and accepted Mr. Arrogant into the family with open arms. They had no idea of what I was going through or had gone through. I did what I needed to do for the army and tried to stay under the radar.

When I got pregnant with my second child, Mr. Arrogant was furious. He did not want me to be pregnant. He didn't care that this was an adjustment for me. I had been working so hard on trying to get higher rank and was doing correspondence courses, trying to max out on everything I possibly could so I could get my E5 sergeant rank. I just needed to go to Primary Leadership Development Course (PLDC) school, but due to the pregnancy I couldn't go.

Mr. Arrogant made the pregnancy difficult. For example, he was invited to a house party on post and he asked me if I wanted to go. Normally I would say no but this time I said yes. He didn't want me to go but he didn't say it. When we got there, he disappeared the whole time, leaving me there with no one to talk to because I didn't know any of his co-workers.

I forgot to mention he got out of the military on an early out and he worked at the Post Exchange. I wanted to go home. He was mad when we left to go pick up the kids. When we got there our son was sleep, he made me carry our son while he took off walking holding his daughter's hand, knowing I wasn't supposed to carry him.

Later I found out he had a girlfriend and she didn't know I was pregnant until I showed up with him being very pregnant. It messed things up for him. We had been getting a lot of calls that

Mr. Arrogant said were the wrong number. I came to find out they weren't the wrong number. It was his girlfriend's husband trying to get in touch with me to let me know what was going on.

I found this information out because Mr. Arrogant had his girlfriend in my car and she had dropped the hotel receipt on the passenger side. It had all her information on it, so I did some investigating and I talked to the girlfriend's husband.

Mr. Arrogant tried to lie his way out of it. He was such a good liar, but I didn't believe a word he said. One day he had disappeared for a whole day. When he got home, we argued. I left the house and stayed away until the wee hours. I had gone to midnight bingo.

When I got home, he was very upset. He wanted to know where I had gone. I wouldn't tell him, and he wouldn't leave me alone about it. I tried to just go to bed but he wouldn't allow that. I was tired and I didn't want to argue with him, yet I still wasn't answering his question of my whereabouts.

Things were really getting heated and I asked him to just leave. He told me I would have to call the police to get him out of the house, so I called the police to get him out.

When the police arrived, he asked what was going on and I told him I just wanted to go to sleep but Mr. Arrogant wouldn't leave me alone. I explained to the officer that Mr. Arrogant said that I would have to call the police to get him to leave.

Mr. Arrogant lied to the police and said I kicked him in the back, and because of the lie I was taken to jail. I asked the police to look at his back to see if there was evidence of me kicking him in the back. The police officer said he wasn't medical so he wouldn't look. He said because this was a domestic feud that one of us was going to go to jail, and it would be me because Mr. Arrogant said I kicked him in the back.

Since I was going to jail for that lie, I was so angry that I really tried to kick him in the back. The police tried to stop me, but I was determined to kick him in the back. Mr. Arrogant told me that if I wake the kids up and they see me going to jail it would scare them, so at that point I cooperated.

I had been talking on the phone to my sergeant who was also my friend. She heard everything, and she bailed me out of jail after I got booked. My chain of command was notified and my sergeant friend who was also in my chain of command had taken charge and I had to stay with her for a week.

Mr. Arrogant had been in trouble with Colorado Springs Police Department for previous assaults on me. He was already supposed to be taking anger management classes, and doing community service, so I guess it was better for him to lie and say I kicked him.

When I met with the prosecutor, he wanted me to take a plea, but instead I told him I would go to trial. He tried to scare me, telling me that if I was found guilty, I could do jail time, but I stood my ground I didn't kick him.

By the time I saw the judge I was really showing and I had bronchitis so I could barely talk. He asked me a few questions and then he dismissed the case.

Life with Mr. Arrogant was like living with a bunch of Sour Patch Kids. One minute he was as sweet as can be, then the next he was awful.

I had finally given birth to my second child. I had to have a C-section. The cut-off score for the E5 sergeant rank had dropped and I made the cut-off score. I couldn't wear the rank until I successfully complete PLDC, but because I had a C-section, I had to wait 6 months before I could go to PLDC.

Meanwhile I got orders to go to Korea and I couldn't take my family. Mr. Arrogant and I talked about him taking the kids and I would send him money. At first, he agreed but then he said no and that he was going back to his home state. He wasn't going to take the kids because he said he needed to find himself. He was leaving me with two kids to manage by myself at a critical time. I begged him to help me out but he wouldn't and left.

At first, I was doing ok, but then I would get assigned longer hours and coming up on the 24-hour roster more. It was too hard. I had gotten permission from the first sergeant to take a three-day pass to drive my kids to Indiana to my mother. Another girl and me drove them to Indiana to my mother.

When I got back, I was trying really hard to get myself ready for PLDC before I had to go to Korea. I knew if I was an E5, those orders for Korea would be revoked because it was slotted for an E4. When I would talk with my mother, she said everything was going well, but one of my aunts called and told me otherwise.

My aunt told me the kids just cried all the time and the kids didn't know any of them. It was true that the kids didn't know my family. They had only talked with my mom on the phone, but they didn't know her. My aunt also stated my mom was on the verge of losing her job because of my kids.

I had to go back to Indiana to get my kids. I was struggling with two kids financially because I had to pay three different sitters to help accommodate being a soldier. I still was being pulled for extended duty, the 24-hour roster at the barracks and 24-hour roster at the hospital.

I was given the extended duty because I was reliable and worked hard. There were soldiers that lived in the barracks that was ate up (slang for screw up) and because of that I was picked to handle a lot of things.

It didn't go unnoticed because there was a female E8 sergeant first class that gave me compliments every time she saw me. She said she needed me to work for her in her clinic. I really tried but I couldn't be a mother and a soldier. My family care plan had failed, and I had to notify my chain of command.

Things got so that I couldn't perform my military duties because I was worried about my kids. The anxiety was so bad. I was going to take my kids and leave the military. That would have been AWOL. I told the staff sergeant in my chain of command that I was leaving now, and he calmed me down and suggested that we go see the first sergeant. In my mind I knew this was going to turn out ugly because of the history with the first sergeant.

At the time the first sergeant was on leave and the acting first sergeant was the E8 that always complimented me on my work ethics. When I told her what was going on, she had me to put it in writing and she started the process for me to get out on a parenthood discharge. She explained to me that it was an honorable discharge.

By the time the first sergeant came back, the process was in motion and he try to change the discharge to general, but he couldn't because I had no article 15 or any negative marks against me. I started outprocessing.

While I was preparing to get out of the service, the wife of Mr. Arrogant's friend, the sergeant that pulled him off me, had asked if she could stay with me until her place was available. I let her stay with me and she offered me encouragement. Mr. Arrogant would call but I wouldn't talk to him. She would try to get me to talk to him but I wouldn't. She would tell me that I was a good mother and a beautiful person. She would tell me to look in the mirror and see it but I couldn't look in the mirror. I hated who I saw in the mirror. I just moved on autopilot and took care of my babies. When movers came to the house and packed all my belongings, she gassed my car up for me.

I drove 18 hours straight from Colorado with my two babies. I only stopped for gas every time the tank was on the half mark. Every time I stopped, I would call a relative to let them know exactly where I was. On one of the stops, I was in an area where black people weren't supposed to be. I knew it immediately. I was so afraid but I had to get gas.

I was in some part of Kansas. I called my grandma's brother and his wife who lived in Kansas. They lived away from the route I was taking. When they found out where I was, they wanted me to come to them. They confirmed I was in a bad area for black people. The gas attendant was really nice, he gave the boys candy and he told me to be very careful.

I didn't go to my grandma's brother house. I continued driving toward Indiana because I already had my route mapped out on the map and I didn't want to take any chance on getting lost. I didn't have any problems on the highway. I believe God was looking out for my babies and me.

My Life After Military Service

I made it home in time to have Thanksgiving with my family. I remember being so anxious about being home that I couldn't sleep after the long drive. One of my aunties and I went to the mall with my kids. I was holding my baby in my arms pushing an empty stroller while we were walking through the mall. A man bumped me really hard and kept walking at a fast pace, immediately my baby started crying. I didn't try to confront the man because he was walking so fast and my focus was consoling my baby.

As I rocked him in my arms and rubbed his head my hand sank down in his head. I started screaming what's wrong with my baby's head, what did he bump us with? I was in panic mode.

My aunt came over to see what was wrong and as she felt his head, she said we have to get him to the hospital. I drove to the emergency room on sheer autopilot; my mind was in and out, and the panic inside had taken over me. I could hear people talking, but I couldn't hear.

When the emergency doctor came out to speak to me, he told me my son had a skull fracture. He questioned me and re-questioned me over and over. He asked me when did I notice his head being soft. I told him after the man in the mall bumped us.

He explained that the fracture was a week or so old. I was in shock and I was crying. I explained to him that I just got out of the military and I had a few different babysitters and none of them said anything about him getting hurt or falling. The emergency room doctor then proceeded to tell me that they have to send him to Indianapolis Children's Hospital and social services were also notified.

I remember crying so hard. I felt like I let my baby down, that I wasn't there for my baby just like my mother wasn't there for me. I felt like my heart was being ripped out of my chest. They made me feel like I was nothing, like I was a criminal.

All the negative words that was said to me over the years came rushing at me all at once again: you will never make it, you're a crybaby, no one is going to want you etc., etc. I was pleading for me and pleading for my baby. I explained to them that I wouldn't hurt my baby, and that I got out the military to take care of my kids.

I tried to contact all the babysitters that I had and questioned them if anything happened while my baby was in their care. I got no answers from any of them. When we got to the Indianapolis

Children's Hospital, the treatment toward me from some of the medical staff was horrific.

I called Mr. Arrogant at the time, crying and begging him to help me. I told him what was going on and that I was afraid that they were going to take my kids away. He assured me that he wouldn't let that happen. I stayed by my baby's side at the hospital the entire time he was there, consoling him and comforting him.

I beat myself up over and over again. How could a mother not know what happened to her child? My family was taking care of my oldest son while I was at the Indianapolis hospital. I spoke with him frequently making sure he was ok, and I told him that I was in the hospital taking care of his brother for now.

I would ask the nurse if she would sit with my baby while I went to the cafeteria to get food and snacks for us or while I went to the bathroom. I explained to her I didn't want my baby left alone at any time. That nurse watched me with my baby and she told me she knew that I didn't hurt my baby. She said that the next time I needed to go to the cafeteria I could take my baby with me.

The next time I went to the cafeteria I took him with me. When I got back, one of the other nurses freaked out on me. She took my son away from me, stating that I shouldn't have taken him with me. I explained to her that I got permission from the other nurse before I took him to the cafeteria.

She took him in the room and examined him, noting that he had bruises on his back and butt. I felt like I was losing my mind but I knew I couldn't show it. I didn't want to be locked up in some psych ward or jail. I felt like it was happening all over again, me being put in the psych ward like while in the military and taken to jail because of lies.

When the doctor came in to examine him, he set the record straight. He said those are not bruises, they are Mongolian spots and explained to the nurse that they are common in black babies. The doctor let me have my baby back.

Some of my family members visited and brought my oldest son to see us. When we finally got released from the hospital, I was told that social services would be visiting us soon and that they will continue on until the case was closed.

I knew I had to act fast because I didn't have a job or a place to stay. My mom lived in the projects/ hood, whatever you want to call it. I knew I couldn't stay with her long; it was against the rules. I had two choices: 1. I could ask the well-known man for financial help in securing my own place, but that would put me back in a situation that I refuse to go back; 2. I could just deal with Mr. Arrogant's abuse, and besides these were his kids, too.

I went to Chicago where Mr. Arrogant lived and I applied for unemployment. I had lots of family in Chicago, but I realized I couldn't live in Chicago. I wanted to be home in Indiana.

I transferred the unemployment to Indiana. I still had to find a place to stay and knew I had to hurry up. Mr. Arrogant helped me secure an apartment in Indiana. He was back in my life and I continue to allow myself to be back in the same situation as before. I just went along with whatever. I just existed at this point.

When I had gotten out of the military, I had filed medical claims for a medical condition that I had been treated for or diagnosed with while I was in the military. I was in excellent condition when I went into the military, but when I got out, I realized those six years in the military took a toll on me and my body.

The VA had scheduled physical and mental examinations. I really needed help mentally for everything I had been through. I didn't trust the VA. They didn't care about me, just like the army didn't care about me, and besides no one ever listened to me.

In my mind the government was just like any other abuser. I held everything together for my kids. I knew that if I didn't, my kids would suffer and I couldn't let my kids down again. I made a promise to my kids. I would do whatever it takes to make sure they had a good childhood and I would be there for them every step of the way. I would be the best mom that I know how to be even if it meant sacrificing me.

The child protection service finally contacted me. They wanted to make a house visit. When the child protective service worker showed up to my apartment, I was watching TV and finishing the last bit of laundry. She noted the house was clean and the kids were well taken care of. After the tour of the apartment, we sat down and talked.

She informed me that she only had one problem and concern. I asked her what was the problem and concern. Her response was, in the kid's room there were no sheets on their beds. I took her to the dryer and opened it and showed her the kids bedding. I explained to her that I could have put other bedding on the bed but the kids had a theme for their room and I wanted to stick with that. I like for things to match. I have to have things matching.

It's funny how my brother and I were taught that everything has to match from his father. Both of us are still like that. To me, the child protective worker was fishing for something to be wrong, but there wasn't and the case had to be closed. If nothing else, I can say I am a good mother.

My boys love their father; sometimes I believed they loved him more than they loved me. They really looked up to him. I continued to stay in the relationship with Mr. Arrogant because of my boys and I felt like I had to. As long as I did what he wanted, Mr. Arrogant would help me out financially and that made it easier for my boys.

I would travel back and forth to Chicago so that the boys could spend time with their father. I was always the one who had to drive to Chicago, Mr. Arrogant always had an excuse why he couldn't come and get them. When I couldn't take the boys to see their father, they would get upset and blame me for them not being able to see their father.

I finally got a job and started going to school. My aunt and my grandmother helped out with babysitting my kids while I worked and went to school. I remember I would cry at night while doing homework or studying for a test. I felt like I couldn't do it. Struggling with migraines and other health issues, school and taking care of two small kids — it was too much.

Somehow, I managed. Only God knows how. I even had a high GPA and I mainly got A's. My finances were a mess, however, and I ended up filing a chapter seven bankruptcy. I hated that but it was necessary.

Things seemed like they should be getting a little easier, right? Wrong. While my kids and I were in the house sleeping early one morning, someone knocked on the door to tell me he hit my parked car and that it was a small scratch. He proceeded to give me a piece a paper with a body shop name and phone number to call to get the repair done and said he would pay for it. I asked him if he had called the police so we can make an accident report. He told me no, because he was in a hurry and he didn't have time, plus he said it was a small scratch.

I went out to look at my car and it was not a small scratch. It was a big dent. I told him we were calling the police and making a police report. I didn't care if he was in a hurry. The police report was made and I turned it into the insurance company.

A couple of weeks later, I was in a major car accident that totaled my car. I saw smoke coming from the car and I tasted blood. I tried to take my seat belt off to get to my kids in the back seat but I was stuck. I started yelling for my oldest son to take his seat belt off and to take his brother's seat belt off. I told him to go and take his brother where all the people were standing, that they would help him.

The next thing I saw, my oldest got out of the car and ran to safety, leaving his brother in his car seat. I was still trying to take my seat belt off yelling for someone to come get my baby out of the car. Out of nowhere my grandma appeared and she was taking my baby out of the car seat.

The ambulance came and I was helped out of the car. My front end of my car was shaped like a J. I went in the ambulance to the hospital and I was checked over. I had bit a hole in my tongue and had broken a bone in my thumb. I wasn't able to work for a month because I was right-handed and my job required me to use my right hand. The insurance company made a settlement with me, and since I was still married, Mr. Arrogant had to sign and agree to the settlement as well.

Now it was time for graduation for me. All the hard work had paid off. This graduation should have been one of the happiest days of my life. It was, in fact, one of the worst days of my life.

When I walked across the stage, I was so proud. As I walked down to return to my seat, Mr. Arrogant jumped in front of me and hugged me and he said he was proud of me.

After everything was over, we met our family in the hallway to have cake and punch. I went to give my family hugs and to thank them for coming. Everyone hugged me except my mother. She was mad at me and walked away.

I tried to chase her down to hug her, but she didn't want me to touch her. She was mad because I didn't hug her when I walked from the stage to my seat. I tried to explain to her that I couldn't hug her at that time because I had to get back to my seat and she said you hugged your husband. I tried to explain to her that he had jumped in front of me and hugged me.

She ruined my special day. All the hard work and my accomplishment meant nothing to me now. She acted horribly and Mr. Arrogant video recorded the whole thing. I was so angry with her that I was willing to move to Chicago with Mr. Arrogant, even though things were just as bad with him.

I did seek mental health treatment from the VA off and on and I was given medication. I was trying to move on with my life but I was struggling. I had ended up pregnant and I had a miscarriage.

I was tired of the roller coaster marriage. My aunt had lent me the money so that I could start divorce proceedings. Mr. Arrogant did not cooperate at all; he wouldn't give the address where he was staying, no kind of information whatsoever. I had to play detective. I got the information and filed for divorce.

When I did, all hell broke loose. His sister was trying to help him take my kids away from me by calling child protection, saying I was unstable and that she feared for her nephew safety. She told them I was taking medication for mental health. The child protection once again opened a case and investigated.

When he came to pick the boys up to take them back to Chicago for visitation, I felt like my heart was being ripped from my chest. When he left with the kids, I attempted suicide using the pills the VA had given me. By the grace of God, I didn't take the whole bottle. In the midst of me taking the pills, God showed me my funeral. My kids were crying and my baby son was inconsolable. It broke my heart to see my kids in so much pain.

I made myself stay up for a couple of days because I knew if I fell asleep, I probably wouldn't have awakened again. I called the divorce off and tried to work things out. We had talked about me moving to Chicago again. He had come clean and told me that he had gotten a woman pregnant and that he didn't want to lose me.

I agreed to move forward with the knowledge of another child with some stipulations. I felt uneasy about moving and staying in this marriage so I prayed about it. I asked God not to let me put my kids in a bad situation. I asked God to give me a sign.

Be careful what you ask for. Mr. Arrogant had found us an apartment. He gave the apartment complex all his information and he told me they were going to call me to get my information. When they called me, I had given them all the information they needed but before the man hung up, he said you all have a beautiful little girl.

I questioned the man and I found out that Mr. Arrogant and his baby mama went to see the apartment together. That was the sign I asked God for. He had already lied and wasn't following any stipulations that we had talked about.

When he had called, I told him what I found out and I told him I wasn't moving to Chicago. He called me all day at work. My supervisor had me to take the call, so he would stop calling. She provided me with a private area where I could talk to him.

I went to see my attorney and told her to proceed with the divorce. I had missed my period and found out I was pregnant and when I had the ultrasound I found out I was pregnant with twins. I was in complete shock but I was excited because I was carrying twins.

When I met with the attorney again, I told her and she said the divorce would have to be put on hold until after the birth of the babies. I contacted him and told him about the twins and that the divorce was on hold until the babies are born.

* * *

He came to visit and he was so caring and loving. He would get me something to drink or eat. I didn't have to really do anything around the house, but by the time he left I started having problems with the babies. I would start bleeding heavily, not like with my first pregnancy when I was in the army. When I was in the army pregnant it was spotting here and there. The bleeding was enough that I had to be put on bed rest until I saw a specialist.

While on bed rest I stayed with my grandmother. She waited on me hand and foot. She spoiled me. Anything I wanted to eat she would cook for me. At night when I couldn't sleep, I would read the Bible. I started reading from the beginning of the Bible because I was unsure of where to start.

While I was reading, I slipped into the place inside of me where it was GOD and me. I couldn't stop reading the Bible. The knowledge that I got was amazing. I didn't have to have a preacher to tell me what the Bible was saying because I understood it.

When I finally saw the specialist, everything looked ok and I was able to resume my usual routine. Mr. Arrogant came around again and I started having the heavy bleeding again. Every time he came around that's what would happen. When he wasn't around, I would be doing fine.

I knew he was into different types of herbs, but it never dawned on me that maybe he was putting something in my drink or food until it was too late. The last time he visited me, he had a strange look on his face when he left. I ended up in full-blown labor.

I called my grandmother to come and sit with my boys while I drove myself to the hospital. When I checked into the hospital, I told them I felt like I was sitting on something. They immediately got me undressed and checked me out. The nurse asked me how I got to the hospital. I told her I drove myself and she was shocked.

They wouldn't let me go to the bathroom and they told me they called the doctor and he was on his way in. I looked at the nurse and asked her what was wrong, and she said just wait until the doctor get here.

The doctor arrived and he told me the bad news. He told me that one of the twin's foot was hanging out and that's what I was sitting on. He was still in the sac; my water had not broken. He explained what they were going to do and that I would feel the worst I ever felt.

This doctor didn't know me, or he wouldn't have made that statement. I didn't think it could be any worse than what I have experienced in my life. My mom showed up and we argued about me signing papers for blood transfusion if I needed one. I refused to sign and she kept telling me to sign it.

The doctor put me in a room where I was turned upside down. They had me on magnesium — I think that's what it was. My sinuses were messed up. I thought I was dying.

The doctor didn't lie, not even a little bit. It was absolutely the worst that I had ever been through. Nothing worked, the baby decided he was coming. I was in so much pain. I delivered my first baby and he didn't make it. They did a cerclage to save the other baby.

They handed me my dead baby, and I cried as I looked at his lifeless body. I was so confused about why they brought me my dead baby. I felt like this was the most horrible thing that they could do. They let me sit with the baby for a while.

Then they put me back in a room, but I wasn't upside down. By the second day, things started going wrong. My water had broken, and I had lost too much blood. I remember telling God, if it is a choice between me and the baby, let me live to take care of my other kids.

The next thing I know, I was giving birth to the other baby. I watched him gasp for air and then he died. I was so exhausted mentally and physically. The doctors told the staff to just let me rest. The whole time I was in the hospital I did not sleep and the doctor and nurse noticed that. They asked me to contact Mr. Arrogant to have him make arrangement for the babies.

I called him and he flat out told me he wasn't doing "shit." My mother handled all the funeral arrangements. I hated it in the hospital: all the nursing personnel, the lab tech, all of them just crept around. The silence was so overwhelming. I felt like I was dying inside. I questioned over and over what is wrong with me? What did I do so wrong to deserve all of this?

I was sent home with antidepressants and sleeping pills. I was screaming on the inside, but no one could hear me. I was being tortured from the inside out. I felt like I couldn't speak. I sat quietly in the dark with tears rolling down my face. My son, Marcese Juan Martin, was born on March 21, 2000, and died the same day. My other son, Desmond Martez Martin, was born March 23, 2000, and died the same day.

I begged God to help me. I told God I was sorry for whatever I did. I begged him to please help. My youngest living son had a birthday coming on March 29. I didn't want him to dread his birthday, so I tried to make it extra special. I threw him the biggest skating party ever and we had a family portrait taken.

No one on the outside knew that I just lost twins. After my son's birthday, I was still mourning the loss of the twins. I would sit in the chair silently crying. My oldest son said to me, "Momma, I know why God took my brothers," he said, "God needed baby angels to watch over us."

I got a call from my attorney; she gave her condolences. She told me that Mr. Arrogant called her, and had told her that I lost the babies, to proceed with the divorce.

She was so angry with him. She told him she doesn't work for him, and that when I was ready, just let her know. She said I could take all the time that I needed. Before she hung up, she

added that I was a good person and that asshole didn't deserve someone like me.

I called him and asked him why he would call my attorney now, when I just lost our babies. I told him he didn't even come and bury our boys. His reply was "that's what you get." *I lost our babies and he said that's what I get.*

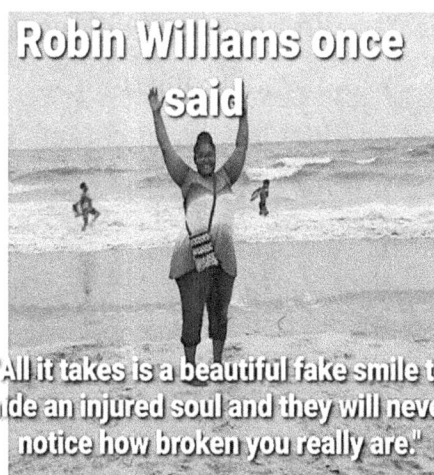
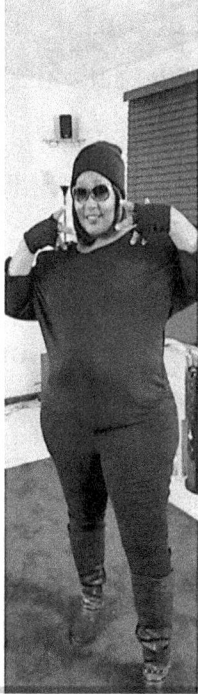

From that moment on, I believed he killed my twins. I wanted revenge for my babies, for me, for everything he had put me through. I remember telling him that one day he is going to regret everything he has done to me.

I was planning to kill him, and my aunt and my cousin stopped me. They prayed and prayed with me for a long time. I cried and I asked God to help me. I didn't go kill him. I decided to let God handle him. Every single day, one of my aunts called me and she always called when I needed comforting the most. She made me laugh and cry all at the same time. She was the one that helped me get through this tough time.

For a long time, I would avoid babies or even looking at them, but you know God has a way of fixing things. I asked for his help and that's just what he did. One day at church, I happened to sit on the opposite side of the church, that was something I never did, but I did that day. I sat behind a church member and her baby, but I wouldn't look at the baby. She had the baby in her baby seat, and she was praising God.

At our church, we believe in shouting/dancing, praising God, whatever you want to call it. Anyway, she was in the front of the church giving God praise. Meanwhile, the baby starts crying and her older sister picked her up, but she couldn't get the baby to stop crying. No ushers came over to help and the little girl looked at me for help. I reached over and took the baby from her, and rocked the baby. The baby stopped crying, but I was silently crying. I had big crocodile tears rolling down my face and they would not stop.

One of the church members, with a pretty voice, started singing a song. She said it was for me, sister Macy. Oh my, that made the tears fall even worst, it was like a flood. I thought we were going to have to build another ark and call it Macy's Ark. From that day forward, I was able to look at, play with, and hold babies.

The hospital called and told me they had my babies' picture and that they were free. I had also received a signed card from the hospital staff. I sent Mr. Arrogant a copy of the picture and the obituary. He was so mad at me, he called and asked why I sent him pictures of dead babies. I told him I thought he would like to have them.

The divorce was soon finalized. I knew that I had to find a way to keep my emotions separate from the kids and their father's relationship. I am not going to lie — it was hard, but I managed. My kids deserved a mother and a father.

I met my second husband at church. We had moved from Muncie to Anderson. I didn't know him long and I did not love him. I married him for the wrong reasons. I married him to piss Mr. Arrogant off. I knew that if I was married that Mr. Arrogant had no right to me. As I said before, it was a possession thing. Well, that didn't work. My second husband knew I didn't love him, and we separated. I got divorced for the second time.

I fell back into the same hole with Mr. Arrogant. I had cheated on my second husband with Mr. Arrogant. That was the only time I was disloyal to anyone. While living in Anderson, I mainly hung around my Pastor from the church I attended — she was also my aunt from my mom's marriage to her nephew. You remember, the one I talked about in the beginning of the book.

I had also met a friend from my kids' school. We later became best friends. I had started writing to God in a journal. I had been writing for a few years here and there. I told God I wasn't ever getting married again unless he sent me a husband and I had to know it was really God that sent him. I told God that the husband that he sent me had to love God and put God first, then me. I told God my husband had to be easy on the eyes and he had to accept all of me. My husband would have to treat my kids like they were his own kids.

Well, I didn't see this coming. I had met this short attractive man that came to church here and there. He caught my attention and I inquired about him. We exchanged numbers but nothing came of it, except we would talk and laugh at church. That was it.

I didn't know that previously he had told one of my cousins that he was going to marry me. It was funny, because my cousin told him I was married to my second husband at the time so he couldn't marry me. Now that I was single, he wasn't. He was engaged to be married.

Another Chance

I didn't hear from him until about a year and half later. He called and said he was no longer engaged — the wedding was off.

We started hanging out. He made me laugh a lot. We were very comfortable around each other. He got to see part of the real me. The fun part. I farted around him and, yes, I said excuse me. He was shocked because most women were not like me. I had told him what you see is what you get.

His job was a few blocks away from my house, so on his lunch break he would call to see if I had cooked. I always cooked because I had kids. I got that from my mom, she always made sure we didn't go hungry when we were little. My mom was a good cook. He would ask if he could come and eat with us. I let him eat with us a few times before I told him that he was going to have to help with groceries. I didn't mind him eating with us, but he was eating with us all the time.

The next time I went to the grocery store he went with me, and he paid half of the grocery bill. He loved my cooking. He was over my house a lot. He would fix things around the house without even being asked. He helped with the utility bill in exchange for him doing his laundry over my house. I watched him around my boys. I loved how he treated them. He would also help them with their homework. He was really good with the boys. My boys seemed to like him a lot as well. That really impressed me.

One day we were sitting on the couch watching a movie and we both fell asleep. His head was on my shoulder when we both awaken; he had drooled all over my shirt while he was asleep. My shirt wasn't a little wet, it was drenched. He was so embarrassed, but I was dying laughing. When I walked him to the door, he kept apologizing to me. Despite his embarrassment he came back over the next day.

When I had to have surgery, he took off work to go to surgery with me. After surgery, when the nurses were trying to bring me out of the sedation, I was fighting everyone and trying to pull everything off me, my mother and him had to help the nursing staff. That was the first time he saw the crazy side of me. That always happened whenever I had surgery. I never understood that at the time but later I found out the reason that always happened.

At home, he took care of my boys and me. He stayed at my house until I recovered. He made sure I had my medication on time, that I was comfortable. He made sure the kids ate and he cleaned around the house.

What? Now who was this man and where did he come from? Come to find out, this man was an old soul trapped in a young man's body. He was old-fashioned, a real gentleman. He and I had gotten really close and we did everything together. We would have the same thoughts; we like to watch the same type of movies and TV shows. He was like a male version of me.

I mentioned him to my best friend and ironically, they had dated in high school. I immediately said, "Oh no, I can't date him." She asked me why and I told her, because you dated him. She laughed and said that was high school, you should date him because he is a good guy.

I continued to date him. My best friend was dating as well and we would hang out and talk about everything except the stuff I had buried deep inside. I had closed all of that off. It was like I erased everything. My best friend married the guy she was seeing and I married my now husband.

We didn't do the traditional marriage process. We had a reception dinner at my house before the wedding. Both sides of the family and me did all the cooking and decorations. My grandmother had asked my husband if he was sure he wanted to marry me and did he know what he was getting himself into. She told him I was crazy.

My marriage at first started off rocky because of trust issues and the wall I had up, but we have stayed together over 15 years. I must say I have the best mother-in-law ever. I told my husband if we were ever to split up that I was keeping my mother-in-law.

Our first year of marriage I got pregnant with my daughter. No, this wasn't a surprise; we planned it. The pregnancy was amazing. I had no problems. I worked all the way up to the delivery date; I work that Friday and on Monday, November 14, 2005, I gave birth to my baby girl by C-section.

Being in the hospital was a challenge for me. I had to hurry up and get out; it was triggering hidden memories. The memories of when the Army had locked me up in the psych ward for six days. The memories of losing my twins.

I had to get out of the hospital. I begged the staff and the doctors to let me out. They finally agreed to let me out earlier than I was supposed to be discharged. I was so scared that I might lose her like I lost my twins, so at home I let her sleep on my chest the whole entire time.

Once while she was on my chest, she was scratching my neck while I was asleep and I freaked out and almost threw her off me, but I awaken up just in time, gasping and holding my baby. That moment took me back to when I was being choked. I had told my husband about it but I didn't tell him about the memory that triggered the responds.

While I was on maternity leave, my aunt would help me with the baby. She would clean the house and keep up my laundry. By the time I went back to work, my baby was attached to my aunt. My aunt took care of my baby, house cleaning and the laundry. When I came home from work, my baby's face would light up, but she wouldn't come to me until my aunt gave the ok. She loved my aunt; my aunt had her spoiled rotten.

The job I had at the time I loved. It was a small group and the people were awesome. It was the best job I ever had. Unfortunately, the business was bought out by another company. I had a gut feeling my company was going to go out of business, so I started looking for another job.

I found a job at a hospital in Indianapolis. When I first started working there, it was good and the department manager looked out for her employees and stood up for us. I loved the work schedule: it was seven on and seven off. The best schedule ever. You work ten hours for seven days and then the next seven days you were off.

I had continued to keep my past buried deep inside. I was existing. I just worked and spent time with my family. The days would go by and I wouldn't have memory of the simplest things.

We lost our manager and had a change in management. The new management didn't really stand up for us, in my opinion, and things went downhill. They were more about self and lacked the understanding of what the staff needed and compassion. Some of the nursing staff were brutal to registration staff; they treated us like we were gum on the bottom of their shoes. They were worse than Cinderella's stepmom and sisters. Don't get me wrong: there were some nice nurses that were amazing.

One day when I was working in the ER, the ambulance had brought a baby in and they were trying to revive the baby. The mother's cry and screams brought me back to the time when I lost my twins. The mother's pleading, begging God and her yelling and crying put me back into that moment. I silently cried at the computer and said a prayer for the mother. I couldn't stop the tears from rolling down my face. I couldn't breathe.

One of the nurses called out, "Macy, can you get the registration information from the mom before the coroner gets here."

She never bothered looking at me, or she would have seen me fall apart right there.

I went to the mother. I said I am so sorry and I asked her if I could give her a hug. I whispered to her that I know the pain that she is feeling that I gave birth to two babies and left the hospital with none. I continued to hug and cried with her. Then I apologized for the intrusion. I explained that I had to get the registration information, and asked whether she was ok with that. I hugged her one last time, then I left the room. The rest of the night was a blur for me.

In 2009, my mother's husband had passed away and it got really crazy. At the hospital, my mom had fainted and hit her head when they told her that her husband had died. She had to be seen in the ER. Some of his kids were making all the decisions on who was going to come get his body, not discussing anything with my mom.

I looked at my mom and I saw how fragile she was. I knew she had a bad heart. I grabbed her and was leaving the hospital with her, when his kids yelled that she can't leave the hospital because she had to sign the hospital papers. They were already making all the decisions without discussing anything with her. I yelled at his kids to leave my mom alone and I was taking her home. I said something in the line of my mother is living and I am trying to keep her alive. I am not fully sure of what came out of my mouth because I went into survival protector mode.

When it came time to make the funeral arrangements and write the obituary, his kids were making all the decisions again, and then they wanted her to sign the papers. My mom had that fragile look again, so I got up and we were leaving, just like at the hospital.

The funeral director called her at home and he asked her how she wanted to handle things. After she told him, he said he would discuss it with my mom's husband's kids.

Everything was handled all wrong. The funeral director was the worst; he had added fuel to the fire. He lied and made things escalate to the point where my mom's stepkids came to her house. They had gotten violent with her; they pulled out a bat and was trying to force their way in. My mom called me frantically and I had to call the police over to her house.

By the time I had gotten to Mom, she was a wreck. I was forced back into the traumatic experience of my childhood mess. I had to help my mom, but I wasn't that helpless child any more. I had been in the military and had enough anger built up inside that I could defend her. I wasn't going to let anyone hurt my mom again.

Before they left, they told my mom to tell me, that I know where they live and to come over there. I was going to go over there but God's voice told me no. I tried to argue with God. Yes, I said I tried to argue with God. In the end I listened. For mom's safety, I helped her get a restraining order against them.

Everything was out of control. At first, we weren't going to let them come to the funeral but they needed to say their goodbyes to their father. They had already lost their mother and I felt bad for them. One of them had showed up with a hammer and had openly made remarks to aggravate me. I went to react but God stopped me once again.

In October 2010, my mom had to have open heart surgery. I would get off work and go to the hospital and stay. I wouldn't leave her side unless she had someone that I trusted to stay with her.

Thank God for my spiritual mother, she would come and stay with my mom so I could go home to shower and get ready for work. I continued to work at the hospital and I advanced in position to become a supervisor. It felt like I was working nonstop, and I wasn't getting enough sleep.

Giving my all wasn't good enough for this job. The staff couldn't get along and we had to fire people, which made my shift even more short of staff. The yelling and screaming at me by staff did not put me in a good place.

My aunt had breast cancer and beat it, but it came back this time she couldn't beat it. My husband had been offered his job, but the only catch was he had to move to another state.

* * *

Let me explain, my husband worked for Guide, which was owned by GM. He didn't take the buyout, so we got to keep all the benefits and GM was supposed to call him back. They would give two offers, you could turn one down but you had to take the second one. He had put in for the Fort Wayne plant or Indiana plant of choice.

They never offered any Indiana plant. If he didn't take the job, we would lose our medical benefits, dental and everything that went along with that job. He waited until the last minute to tell me that he had gotten the second offer and it was out of state. He just didn't want to add onto my pile. I was dealing with the death of my aunt and the funeral stuff. My aunt had left me in charge of handling the arrangements.

My husband was already working a job but he wasn't happy. He had always told me that his dream job was working in a GM factory. This had been his dream since the second grade.

I looked my husband in his eyes and saw what this job meant to him. Everyone else told him not to take the job. They told him he should stay here with his family. I convinced him to go take the job and that we would figure it out. I prayed to God to help me because I didn't know how I was going to handle all of this. Having a husband six hours away was going to be challenging, especially since I have trust issues. Nevertheless, I started researching the area and making phone calls to find an apartment for my husband to stay in.

Another Chance

I know God answered my prayers because everything just fell in place. My husband stayed one night with a relative and by the time he got off work that day I had found him a studio apartment in a really nice area in Ohio. He was able to move in. The property manager had to be an angel in disguise; she and I coordinated everything over the phone.

My daughter was struggling with the loss of my aunt. She wanted more of my attention. Mentally I was in a bad place. The migraines were unbearable. I was exhausted trying to maintain. I knew I had to be there for my daughter. I had made a promise to always be there for my kids.

Eventually I resigned from the job at the hospital. I couldn't do it anymore and I was in a really bad place. Financially I knew it was going to be hard, but my priority had to be my kids and me.

After I resigned from my job at the hospital, my daughter and I went to Ohio for about a month. My husband and I were trying to decide on what to do as far as moving. In the end we decided that he would stay in the apartment and I would maintain our house in Anderson, Indiana.

My daughter and I came back to Anderson. My husband drove every single weekend from Ohio to Anderson, about six hours one way. He did that drive faithfully. He didn't have much of a life in Ohio because he worked third shift and slept all day and then weekend, he was on the highway. He said he rather not have his wife and daughter on the highway. He said he would come to us.

I must admit it was financially difficult. We had an apartment and a house to maintain, not to mention car repairs. We ended up filing chapter 13 bankruptcy. My husband's car completely broke down. I did not know how we were going to make ends meet. We did not qualify for any assistance.

I felt like I was a failure. Everyone looking on the outside didn't have a clue that things were really bad. The thought of suicide was so strong but my faith in God was just as strong. I cried out to God for help. I begged God to make it go away. God is amazing. We were able to find a car that we could pay cash for and it had low mileage. After paying the mortgage and apartment rent there was very little money. Sometimes my mom would cook and invite us over. I never told her how tight things were but deep down I think she knew and that was her way of helping me.

I reached out to the VA to help me find a job. I enrolled in vocational rehabilitation. They arrange for me to work 25 hours a week with the county office and I had to agree to go to all my VA appointments.

I started going to mental health counseling through the VA, at first it was difficult. I didn't trust anyone. I was constantly on high alert as if something was about to happen. The doctor labeled me as bipolar. I didn't agree with her and I didn't like that diagnosis. I felt it was wrong. She wanted me to take medication and said that was the only way I would be able to function, and that it would help me with the migraines and insomnia.

She prescribed me the medication and I took it. I was sort of scared to take it because that's the same medication I tried to commit suicide with. The psychiatrist would order blood work and slowly increase the medication until it was at the levels she wanted me at.

The medication did help with sleep and the migraines to an extent until one day I was awakened with severe abdominal pain that wouldn't stop. I got up to go to the bathroom and when I looked in the mirror my lips and face was swollen like I had been beaten. I went to the emergency room because the abdominal pain was so severe. I was having a reaction to the medication and I had to be weaned off of it. I did not want to try any other medication, but I agreed that I would do mental health therapy.

* * *

On October 1, 2014, the day before my birthday, I got a call telling me my biological father had died. I was devastated. Over the years I reached out to my father but it didn't always turn out so well, because I was so angry at him. I felt like he didn't love me and I wasn't good enough for him. It had gotten to the point that we didn't talk at all. I had told myself that I didn't care anyway, but I did care.

The pain of not having the love of your parent cuts so deep. As my daughter was getting older, she wanted to know about my father and my sisters. She wanted to meet them. I reached out to one of my half-sisters. My family met with my siblings at a restaurant. My boys and my daughter got to meet their aunts. We took pictures together and laughed a lot.

After that meeting, one of the siblings and I kept in touch, for the most part. I had asked her continuously to set something up with our father so my daughter could meet him. It never happened. I don't think he wanted to meet with me; she never said it but that's what I sensed.

I never got to mend things before he died. I realized the mistake I had made: I let the anger stop me from moving forward with a positive relationship with my father. The saying "hurt people, hurt people" is so true. That was a lesson learned the hard way.

I went to the funeral but I left immediately after. I was hurting and I felt broken into pieces. I couldn't let my kids and my husband see me that way. I always put up a front like nothing fazed me. They have never seen that side of me. I continued on as if nothing was wrong. I was a pro at masking all my pain. I was good at that; I had lots of practice.

* * *

I soon got a full-time job working as a Veterans Service Officer (VSO). I did not know that taking the position would cause me so much hostility. I was talked about, lied on, yelled at and called names. It was exhausting.

Not long after that, the psychiatrist and the therapist that I was seeing retired and I was assigned a new therapist. I didn't care much because I didn't have a connection with either of them. I met the new therapist I was assigned, then I disappeared for a little bit, but I eventually went back to her. I didn't trust anyone.

I had already had a bad experience with the VA provider. The neurologist that I seen had been experimenting with different medications to stop the migraines, and ultimately, ended up heavily medicating me to the point where I was having trouble functioning. I was forgetting the simple things and having trouble with words. When I address the concerns with him, he told me I was crazy and I needed to go get mental health. He said my chart says that I was bipolar and I told him that wasn't true.

Later on, I found out the VA let him go because he almost killed someone by overdosing them with medication. I overheard the person telling someone she just got out of the hospital and we started talking and I told her my experience with that particular doctor as well. I got passed around to a couple other neurologists, and long story short, I gave up dealing with VA neurologist.

When I returned to the new therapist, there was something about her and I continued going to her. It took me a long time to open up to her and trust her but I finally did. I felt comfortable with her and I began sharing everything with her. She really understood me. She knew when to push and when to back off.

Mom

In 2016, I almost lost my mother. I had visited my mom while she was in the hospital. Everything, I thought, was going ok. They had changed the medication that they were giving to her and she was going to have some more tests done the next day. Before I left her, I told her I would check on her tomorrow.

The next day, I called her room but I got no answer. I kept calling and calling but still no answer, so I called my oldest son to see if he had visited her. He worked third shift; he had said he was going to go see her when he got off work.

When I talked to him, I had asked if he went to see his grandmother, he said yes. I then asked was she ok, he said yes, she just seemed really sleepy. I still felt uneasy. I had already started putting on my shoes and getting my car keys, when my son stated that the nurse did tell him to let them know when he left because my mom couldn't be left alone.

Instantly, a red flag went up in my head. I asked why she couldn't be left alone. He said he didn't know why. I hung up and started getting into my car, when I received a call from the hospital. They wanted me to come to the hospital because my mother had taken a turn for the worst. I told them I was on my way as we were speaking, then hung up.

I was holding the steering wheel so tightly that when I opened my hands, they were white. Shortly after that I got a call again from the hospital, while I was driving. The doctor told me not to panic; the person that called did not relay that information correctly. He stated that they need to do a procedure, but my mom wasn't coherent enough to give the consent, so they wanted me to come to give the consent.

Before I went into the hospital, I went on Facebook and asked my family to pray for my mom. I knew Facebook would be the quickest way to reach my family. I didn't have time to try to call them, and I didn't know everyone's number. Some of them changed their number just like they changed their drawers.

When I saw the doctor, it was much more serious than he had led me to believe over the phone. He only did that because he did not want me to panic and have an accident trying to get to the hospital.

I couldn't breathe, I couldn't speak. I just froze in place. My aunt, (the one that prayed with me and stopped me from going to go after Mr. Arrogant when I lost my twins) was suddenly beside me, telling me to sign the consent so they could place a line in her neck. They needed to get medicine to her heart immediately and then they were going to life line her to Indianapolis heart hospital.

I asked the doctor to let us see her, before they did the procedure and he did. She knew who we were and that made me feel a little better. The doctor said it would not take long and he would come get us when he was done.

It was taking a long time. I started to worry. When I called and asked what was wrong, they told me that the doctor will be out to talk with me in a little while. My mom did not do well with the procedure, and they could no longer life line her using the helicopter. She would have to go by ambulance because of the state she was in.

I rode in the front seat of the ambulance and was having an anxiety attack. I started doing some of the breathing exercises that my therapist taught me. I kept doing those breathing exercises over and over again.

We finally arrived at the heart hospital. They took her into the emergency department and asked me to wait in the waiting room. Family members had arrived and joined me in the waiting room. They were asking me questions, but I couldn't answer anything.

One of the doctors came into the waiting room and asked for me. He told me my mom was in really bad shape and might not make it. I cried out loud, hysterically begging him to save my mom. I looked at him, crying, begging, screaming "please save my mom, please I don't have anyone. She is all I have. Please you don't understand please, please save her." I said all of this without taking a breath.

I cried so hard that the doctor had tears in his eyes. He finally said, "I will do everything I can," and told me to just pray because it is all up to God. As the doctor left the room, I stood there feeling helpless.

I heard one of my aunts say, "Macy just let her go." I yelled NO. I went to sit down. There was no one that came to hug me. I felt that loneliness right to my core. I honestly don't know if I would have been able to feel it any way, if someone had hugged me. I know that sounds weird.

There have only been a couple of people that hugged me in a way where I felt their warmth reach all the way to my core. Where I felt like I could stay in their arms forever, let everything out and cry openly. Of course, I never did that with them. I was accustomed to dealing with things on my own.

Our family always had problem with showing affection. I went into my happy place inside of me, where I knew I could talk to God. My conversation in the happy place with God went like this:

> *"God, I am sorry for whatever I did to deserve this. I have always been kind and caring to everyone. I have tried to do everything that you asked of me. God, please, don't take my mom. You already have*

my babies and my biological father, please don't take her, not now. I can't handle it right now. I am asking you, begging you, to let her live, please do it for me. I know you can, you can do anything. I trust you and I love you."

I continued to just sit quietly letting the tears run down my face. I am not sure how much time passed before the doctor returned. He had said they had done all that they could do for her; we will have to see if she makes it through the night. I thanked him and he left.

The waiting room was like a sleepover party. Family was stretched out everywhere. The next day (the aroma from the farts and the funky breath had me scared that the hazmat team was going to be called…I am just kidding), my mom had made it through the night and I thanked God. They had moved mom to the ICU floor.

We were eventually allowed to see her. I think it was no more than two at a time. My mom had a team of doctors. I am sure she had a doctor for every organ of her body (heart doctor, kidney doctor, neurologist). You name it, she had it.

I stayed by her side the entire time. I could hear the nurses whispering. It was just like when I lost my twins. I hated the eerie feeling. My mom was later moved to another floor, where I was able to sleep in her room with her.

I am not sure how long she stayed in ICU. I lost track of time. My husband brought me clothes, personal hygiene stuff, so that I could keep up on my personal hygiene. One of the nurses said if I wanted to, I could put on music. We found a gospel station that I thought mom would like. As the music played softly, I watch the nurse as she watched me. I saw the pity in her eyes but I ignored it. I just kept focusing on my mom, coaching her to stay with me.

Every once in a while, I would see her body kind of twitch, I would get happy. The nurse had called me just outside the door of my mom's room. She told me softly, that the movements my mom was having didn't mean anything — the body sometimes does that. She said she hated to see me get my hopes up high and then be let down. I said ok, and went back into the room.

The people at the job that I had at the time were very understanding. They worked with me to help me in getting FMLA in place. When mom's baby sister came in the room to sit with mom and me, she noticed the movement as well. I told her what the nurse had told me but neither one of us believed what the nurse had said.

After the neurologist saw my mom, he told me he didn't think that there was any brain damage. He would know more when she comes to. He was a little concerned that she had not responded yet, but he said he believe it was due to all the pain medication that needed to get out of her system.

From that point on, I wouldn't let any of the nurses give my mom pain medicine. They could give her all the other medicine, but I refused to let them give her pain medicine. That night, while watching her, I prayed to God asking him to heal her. I rubbed my hands over her forehead and head asking God to restore her back to herself. I asked for complete healing. I told God I would do whatever was asked of me. I vowed I would write to him like I used to, and I would let people know that he was real. I told God by saving and restoring her then people would see the miracle that only God can do.

As I sat there watching my mom it seemed like she was having more movement. I told the nurse that it looks like my mom was using her tongue to try and push the tube from down her throat. The nurse had assured me that would be impossible for her to push the tube out. All night long I was convinced that my mom was actually pushing the tube out with her tongue.

The respiratory therapist came to suction the tube or what ever they do. She was alarmed, and the next thing I knew, all the doctors and nurses came rushing in the room. The respiratory therapist reported to the staff that the tube was out. She wasn't sure how long it's been out. It looked like my mom had been breathing on her own.

The doctor said not to do anything lets just see how she does. Oh, my gosh, when mom started to come to it reminded me of the dry bone's scripters in Ezekiel. She was squirming around;

she wouldn't sit still. She was worse than a two-year-old hyped up on a bag of Halloween candy.

I went from calling her Mom to Houdini. I called her Houdini because she managed to escape anything they used to restrain her. It got to be quite comical, so when one of the nurses and a nursing student got into an argument in front of us, I didn't even get mad. Telling my mom to do something or stop doing something was like talking to a brick wall, she would respond ok but continued to do whatever you told her not to do.

She wanted to eat but she had to wait until speech therapy evaluated her on eating and drinking. The speech therapist started off by giving her a small graham cracker, instructing Houdini to take small bites and to chew so many times before swallowing. Houdini took that graham cracker and it disappeared in her mouth so fast. We had to tell her again to take small bites and chew so many times before swallowing. The speech therapist explained to her that she didn't want her to choke. Houdini said she understood, but again the graham cracker disappeared fast into her mouth. The same thing happened when she was to take small sips of water: she gulped that water down. There was no sipping.

Mom's improvement was coming along quite nicely. The hospital discharged her to a rehab facility in Anderson, the Indiana city where she lived. I went back to work, but I would go to the rehab everyday to see her. When I went to see her one day, she was really sad. I hate seeing her sad. I asked her what was wrong, she said she was tired of just sitting in the room and she missed Lacy. Lacy is her dog.

I asked the staff if I could wheel her outside around the hospital. I had my husband to go get her dog from the house and bring Lacy to the hospital. It was priceless seeing her cry while she held her dog.

After approximately three weeks in the rehab facility she was able to go home. It was rough for me at first, because I had to make food for her, until she was fully capable of making her own food. I had to teach her how to prepare her food, because her eating had to drastically change. It took much longer at grocery stores because we had to look for no sodium or low sodium food. We also had to watch her potassium intake.

*　*　*

My mom was doing better, but I wasn't. The job I had helping veterans didn't feel safe anymore. People were being aggressive and verbally abusive. The feeling of being on high alert was exhausting. I felt like life was being drained out of me. There was no pause, rewind, or fast forward button. Life was still happening. My daughter was struggling with extreme social anxiety.

I quit my job in March 2018, because my daughter and I were both struggling. The suicide thoughts were smacking me in the face, before I could even get my head off the pillow. I knew I had to pull it together for her and get her some help. I would never let my kids down. I made that promise to myself.

I had gotten my daughter in to see a mental health therapist, and I was still seeing my therapist at the VA. On October 2, 2018, my daughter was contemplating on committing suicide. The only thing that stopped her was it was my birthday and she didn't want me to be sad on my birthday. She had been texting me while she was attending an after-school program, she was in crisis mode. My phone was on the charger and I didn't hear the notification. I had always responded to her when she had an episode, so when I didn't respond she didn't know what to do.

When I picked her up from school, she told me that she was going to jump off the second floor to kill herself. Luckily, her best friend/sister was there to help her. I say best friend/sister because they have been friends since the second grade and we sort of adopted her as our child.

My daughter had a situation that she thought she had handled the right way by being honest. You see, my daughter has autism (Asperger's) as well as anxiety disorder. She tried to hide things the best that she could, because she didn't want others to know. She heard other kids making fun of kids with autism.

No one knew my daughter had these conditions, but I knew something was off ever since she was a toddler. She started off being home schooled and I didn't think things would be a problem for her because she was high functioning. I reached out to the school when her condition reared its ugly head. I was told by several people that the school could help and could have her tested. There were programs in place for kids like her.

I met with several members of the school staff before school started to discuss the situation with them about my daughter. At first, they were reluctant to help us because her grades were fine, and they said she seemed fine. The school told me that they needed a medical diagnosis. I would have to have her tested and provide them with documentation. I found a facility that test for autism and it was confirmed that she had autism.

The payment for that type of service was not covered by our insurance, so we had to pay out of pocket. It was expensive but due to error in their billing department they had to write the cost off. God was still looking out for me.

Despite me getting everything the school asked for, they still turned her down for services. I had to get the state involved, then that's when the school started to help. The state got us into a program called wraparound service. It was an amazing service. This was a lot of work and persistence on my part to get to this point.

The combination of the wraparound services and her therapist helped my daughter open up more. They helped my family put a safety plan in place for my daughter. My daughter doesn't mimic others any more in order to get by. I have been working with her on accepting who she is, and to always be true to herself. She hates that autism is called a disability, so I told her not to think of it as a disability but more of an ability. I told her she has abilities that other people don't have and that is special, and it makes her special.

My husband was having a hard time understanding that his wife and daughter were having mental issues. Usually when we are having an anxiety attack, he would make things worse. One time when we went into a crowded grocery store, both of us had an anxiety attack. My husband was being impatient with us and making things worse. My daughter put her headphones on, and I was losing it by the second. A voice in my head said run him over with the shopping cart. I looked at my daughter and I said, "I am gonna run him over with the cart." She shrugged her shoulders and said ok.

I went racing down the aisle and ran into the back of his shoe with the cart. There was a man that watched everything. The expression on the man's face was priceless! Watching my husband's face and him trying not to fall caused my daughter and me to laugh uncontrollably. It was like watching him trying to dance. We were laughing so hard that we were crying. That made us feel better, but my husband wasn't too happy. We laughed all the way home; he still wasn't too happy. I find that in the middle of an anxiety attack that if I can get my mind on something else or find something funny it helps me recover faster.

I know running my husband over with the cart may sound cruel, but it wasn't: I would not do anything to hurt anyone I love. It was like you letting your small child push the cart and they run over the back of your shoe. Having a playful husband sometimes help with anxiety.

Sometimes my husband and I are like two big kids left unsupervised. My daughter often refers to us as a five-year-old and a three-year-old. Of course, I am the five-year-old. I am so thankful for my adoptive daughter. When I am not around, she helps my daughter with her anxiety. Once when our adoptive daughter was over to the house and my husband and I weren't behaving like adults, my daughter starts crying saying why can't I have normal parents.

Our adoptive daughter hugged and consoled our daughter telling her, it's ok, buddy. My husband and I laughed so hard. You couldn't possibly blame us for laughing. Our daughter would refer to us as my mother, father or parental unit, so we would tease each other and call each other mother and father. We really did sound like two toddlers going back and forth. My family and our adoptive daughter's family are close. We take our adoptive daughter on vacations with us because it helps our daughter and we enjoy her company.

* * *

I had been talking with my half-sisters off and on. We had talked about vacations and having a girl's day out. I had invited my siblings over to watch a movie and dinner. I had asked if one of them would be willing to do a DNA test with me. I wanted to clear any doubt that anyone might have about my biological father being my father, so I paid for a DNA test for my baby sister and me.

In March 2019 I got the DNA test back. My biological father was exactly who my mother said he was. That should have made me feel better, but I was sad because it hurt my mom. She told me she wouldn't lie to me about something like that.

I wish she had of taken a DNA test with my father when I was born. I told her that it's not fair to the child to have to verify who their father was. My mom said she did go uptown to the child support division, but she was threatened by my biological father's brother, so she left it alone.

* * *

At this point you would think life would give me a break right. Nope. In January 2020 I got a call to come to the hospital because the doctor needed permission to take my father off life support. I was in total shock. I left my husband and my daughter at home and drove myself to the hospital. All I saw is this man that always made me feel like I belong, the man that wanted to adopt me as his own daughter lying in the hospital bed with a tube in his mouth lifeless.

I lost it, I cried and beg the doctors to save him. The doctor kept insisting that there was nothing more they could do. I tried to close my emotions off, but I couldn't, I paced the floor begging God to let him live. I kept seeing flashbacks of my mother lying in bed lifeless, when I almost lost her four years ago. I couldn't breathe. I kept trying to coach him to come back to this side of the world. I cried and held his hand asking him not to leave. I couldn't reach him. He was too far gone.

I stayed at the hospital for hours, then I called my best friend and asked her to help me find his biological daughter. Like always, my best friend came through. I called my little sister and told her that her dad is on life support and that the hospital wants to take him off life support, but I wouldn't let them. I told her that was her call to make. I felt so bad telling her over the phone, but she was in another state and I had no choice.

It hit me again, the thought that I didn't belong to anyone, and I was by myself. The feeling of emptiness never goes away. When I went home, I shut down and went into myself. I did nothing all day, then the next day I went to work. I pretended like none of this happened. I was very irritable and anxious.

My little sister finally arrived in Anderson. I left her to handle all the arrangements for her father. She did an amazing job. I was so proud of her.

During the funeral service, one of my mom's stepdaughters from her deceased husband showed up at the funeral to pass a card to me and then she left. I didn't open the card at the service.

Me: The Good, the Bad, the Ugly and the Survival

I was trying so hard to be strong for my baby sister even though we weren't biological sisters. I still felt like she was my baby sister.

After the funeral service, on our way to the restaurant where we were to meet my baby sister, I open the card that my mom's stepdaughter gave to me. I was so furious that someone would stoop so low to send a card to me, trying to hurt me. I called my therapist's office, and once again she helped me not fly off the handle. I thought again about the saying "hurt people, hurt people." I thought about reaching out to my mom's stepkids but I didn't. If writing me this card makes her feel better than I will let her have that and I pray that God remove the hurt. I wish the best for her.

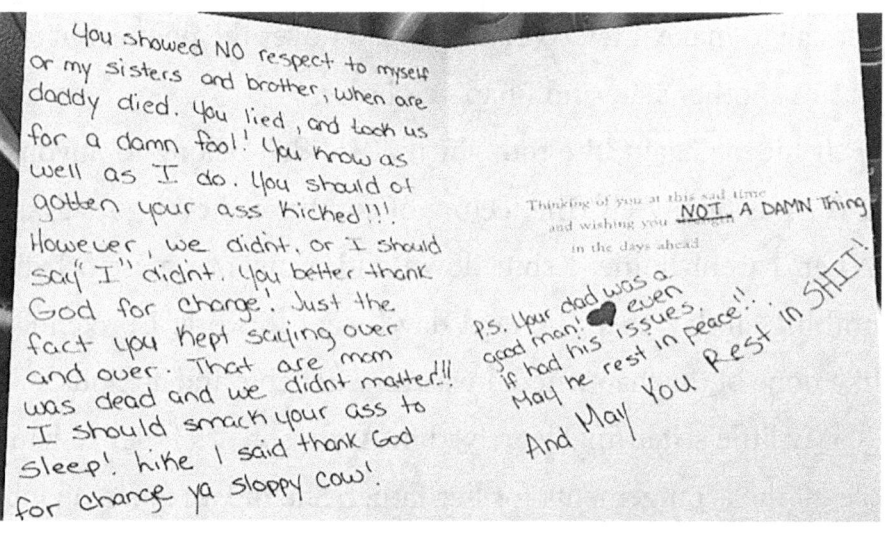

The Will to Live

In the beginning of this book, I stated that having a good therapist was a must when dealing with trauma and the healing process. The struggle to live became much more intense for me, when my therapist of four years decided to move on to bigger and better things. I no longer had my therapist. The therapist that had guided and coached me every step of the way would no longer be there for me. I was dealing with being on lockdown for weeks, then months because of Covid-19, the race issues, the riots — all the things going on in the world on top of my inner war.

I honestly felt like I couldn't win. I felt like giving up and the feeling of ending it rose in me like a blazing wildfire. The constant panic attacks, the difficult breathing was consuming me. In my head I kept telling myself over, and over again: I don't want to die, I don't want to die, I don't want to die.

As I looked around, I tried to feel the love and warmth from my family and friends. I felt like I was sinking in quicksand, returning to that dark room that I was in with no windows. I kept trying to hide how I was feeling from my family and friends by isolating myself. All the reserve energy I had was depleted. I had to pull it together somehow, for me, for my daughter, for my family, for all the victims of trauma, of life.

I prayed, cried and begged God to help me. I could hear the verse from the Bible being whispered ever so softly. You can do all things through Christ that strengthens me. You can do all things through Christ that strengthens me.

My therapist had told me several times that avoidance makes things worse. It was time for me to use everything that my therapist had taught me. The breathing exercise, the focus on staying grounded. It was time. I know it's not going to be easy, the urge to just give up will probably come up more than once. Just like a recovering addict, I will have to take it one day at a time. If I mess up, it's okay. I don't have to beat myself up; life has done enough of that.

I have a tall mirror on the wall outside my bedroom door, with tiny mirrors surrounding it, with a message that says, "BE KIND TO YOURSELF." I know, I will have to tend to that lost me with gentle hands just like I would tend to an infant or a wounded person.

My Revelation

I always thought I didn't belong to anyone, that I wasn't even good enough for my mom to love me, or for my biological father to love me and be in my life. I was wrong, my mom loves me in her own way, and every once in a while, I would get a glimpse of her being proud of me.

Trauma distorts things. As for my biological father, it was his loss that he didn't get to see how amazing I am, and how smart and talented his grandkids are before he died. I am not saying this in an arrogant way, I am saying it in a humble way.

When I really look at things deeply, I must admit I have been truly blessed from the day I was born. When I hear my mom say that when I was born, she could of died, I could have died or we both could of died from me being born breach — butt first, I realized that I was special, unique.

God spared my life. The unconditional love that I have always searched for was right in front of me, but I just didn't know it. God always had unconditional love for me and was always there for me, but I didn't have unconditional love for myself. I now know that I would have to love myself no matter what. I would have to love the good qualities as well as the bad qualities, understanding that I will never be perfect, no body's perfect.

The realization that I had 3 fathers also hit me: my biological father who gave me life, the father that wanted to adopt me, taught me love and compassion, and the well-known man taught me everything else, the good and the bad. I don't hate the well-known man. Yes, I hate what he did, and I will always have scars from that part of my life. That's something I will never get rid of.

The first step in loving me, is taking care of me. It is time to put me first. When I used to hear people say I am putting me first, I used to think they were being selfish, but now I understand. It's not being selfish to tend to your well-being, and to set boundaries for others.

I have learned that people will take from you and abuse you, as long as you allow them to. They will take you for granted. It's not just people; it's also jobs. Jobs that have you working 12 hours with no break, they don't care about you. I am learning my self-worth, so that when I am around toxic people or toxic jobs, I don't have to stick around to take the abuse.

Life has taught me so much, it's like a big school (University of Life), and to think I thought I was done with school. One of the life's lessons from the University of Life is that some people were meant to stay in your life, those are the ones that truly love you, and some were meant to leave your life.

My Revelation

To the ones that stayed in my life, *Thank You*. To the ones that left my life, I want to say *Thank You* as well. I say that because either you were a blessing or a lesson. Both blessing and lessons are what made "ME." Last, but not least, always surround yourself with positive energy.

ME (Lyrics)

By Macy Fuller

To listen to the song, go to my website:
www.MacyFuller.com/music

I wanna be me (just let me be)

I wanna be free (just let me be)

I wanna breathe

I need to breathe

Inside my head I tried to figure it out

No one around no one to help me out

So all alone in this cold, cold world

A small child

I was just a little girl

Inside my mind I tried to block things out (block things out)

The lies the secrets that could never be told (never be told)

Shattered dreams

I had to keep it inside

Inside of me

I wanna be me (just let me be)

I wanna be free (just let me be)

I wanna breathe

I need to breathe

I wanna be me (just let me be)

I wanna be free (just let me be)

I wanna breathe

I need to breathe

Inside my heart I know I will never be the same (never be the same)

The hurt the shame that takes over me (over me)

How could this be how could this happen to me (happen to me)

A small child

I was just a little girl

A small child

I was just a little girl

I wanna be me (just let me be)

I wanna be free (just let me be)

I wanna breathe

I need to breathe

I wanna be me (just let me be)

I wanna be free (just let me be)

I wanna breathe

I need to breathe

www.ingramcontent.com/pod-product-compliance
Lightning Source LLC
Chambersburg PA
CBHW070111080526
44586CB00013B/1267